Setting Psychological Boundaries

Setting Psychological Boundaries

A Handbook for Women

Anne Cope Wallace

BERGIN & GARVEY
Westport, Connecticut • London

Library of Congress Cataloging-in-Publication Data

Wallace, Anne Cope.
    Setting psychological boundaries : a handbook for women / Anne
Cope Wallace.
      p. cm.
    Includes bibliographical references and index.
    ISBN 0–89789–534–7 (alk. paper)
    1. Personal space—Psychological aspects. 2. Boundaries—
Psychological aspects. 3. Women—Psychology. 4. Interpersonal
relations. I. Title.
BF697.W28   1997
158.2—DC21   97–10407

British Library Cataloguing in Publication Data is available.

Library of Congress Catalog Card Number: 97–10407
ISBN: 0–89789–534–7

First published in 1997

Bergin & Garvey, 88 Post Road West, Westport, CT 06881
An imprint of Greenwood Publishing Group, Inc.

Internal design and typesetting: Letra Libre

Printed in the United States of America

The paper used in this book complies with the
Permanent Paper Standard issued by the National
Information Standards Organization (Z39.48–1984).

10 9 8 7 6 5 4 3 2 1

This book is dedicated to the women everywhere who inhabit "green rooms of my life."

In particular, I want to dedicate this work to my grandmother, Annie Mae, my mother, Kathleen, and my father, Robert E. Lee, who gave me my first love of the spoken and the written word, and to my three children, Jamie, Allison, and Edward, whose unconditional belief in me as a writer has sustained me during the dry seasons.

Contents

Acknowledgments

First, I would like to thank the subjects of my study, whose candor, passion, and understanding have made this work possible. Their names, descriptions, and geographic settings have been changed to preserve confidentiality.

My agent, Nancy Lacey, has given me great gifts of sustained enthusiasm, encouragement, and professional guidance in the realization of my book. Thank you, Nancy!

My friend and fellow writer, Sondra Gash, has worked with me from the early stages of producing the manuscript, and her encouragement and commitment to the study; her sharp eye for organization, and clarity; and her appreciation for music and metaphor have enabled me to put the pieces together. I would also like to thank my friend and fellow poet, Barbara Morcheles, whose editorial input and counsel have been invaluable.

To family therapist, Pamela Day, I owe a large debt for her time and professional expertise in family systems therapy and for the psychological questionnaire that became the basis for my interviews. I am more than grateful to friend and psychologist, Laurie Lidner, for her enthusiasm, counsel, and the professional references she so willingly provided me.

I want to thank all of the friends who have surrounded me with support and enthusiasm for this project, especially Joan Pittis, Nancy Andrews, Kim and Jay Rippard, Anne Hansen, and Pauline Strahman.

My gratitude also goes to my husband, Ned, for his patience in living with that strange species—a writer—and to my children, Jamie, Allison, and Edward, for their sustained encouragement.

Finally, I want to thank the editors at Greenwood Publishing Group, particularly Nita Romer, Ellen Louer, and Norine Mudrick, for their faith in my work and their love of the symbol as well as the song.

All of the poems included in the book are my own, with the exception of the symbolic poem "Keeping Silent" by Nancy Ornstein and the emotionally powerful "At the Lake" by "Barbara." I am most grateful to both Nancy and Barbara for the use of their imaginative works.

Introduction

Pioneering family therapist, Salvador Minuchin, defines *psychological boundaries* as "the invisible barriers that protect the integrity and rights of the individual." On first discovering this interpretation of the dynamics of interpersonal relationships, I was intrigued with the possibilities for change that such a concept might bring to my life and the lives of others. For we deal with *violations of the self* or *boundary invasions* daily—overt and covert attacks on our self-esteem, our sexuality, our bodies; intrusions on our privacy, our possessions.

I believe that in recognizing and respecting our boundaries we affirm ourselves, our rights in all our relationships, and the rights of others. When we fail to defend ourselves, when we fail to stand up for ourselves under attack, we lose some treasured part of ourselves— our integrity, belief in ourselves, the real "I" at the core of the inner self, and each time this is a little death. And when we fail to respect the rights of others, we inflict losses, large and small, that may shake the core of lives of all we touch.

I have written this book for women because, first of all, being a woman, I speak from a woman's perspective, I see and hear as a woman, I feel as a woman. And although psychological boundaries are just as important to men in building healthy flexible relationships, I write for women because we, traditionally and culturally, have held positions of diminished power in our society.

A great influence in our skewed heritage as women, I believe, is in our history and tradition. For up until the twentieth century women enjoyed few rights, and even now, with the growing momentum of the women's movement, we still suffer from the image that a patriarchal society has instilled in us—our role as submissive, self-sacrificing human beings. It is a given that we continue to have problems believing we can express what we feel, think, want, and in remembering that we do have choices.

Recognizing that continued violations of boundaries have tremendous repercussions for all of us, I set out to explore the link between childhood experiences and boundary violations. I began researching boundary and victimization issues under the guidance of Pamela S. Day, practicing family therapist, who suggested a battery of twenty-five questions that became the basis for my data. And although the participants in my study were not chosen scientifically, but were brought to me by a network of friends, colleagues, and organizations, I don't think I could have selected a more diverse group in terms of demographics, culture, family background, economic status, talents, and interests. The only real connection between them is that they have all suffered difficult—and sometimes severely dysfunctional—childhoods or destructive marital relationships.

As my research progressed, I became concerned not just with the impact of family patterns on our adult lives but with the resolutions and the means for moving away from unhealthy behavioral patterns, how to overcome our losses, fears, anxiety, and dependency. I wanted to know how we, as adult women, become all that we are capable of becoming; what are the paths that have taken us to where we are today, and was the path easy or difficult? Is there hope in the struggle, optimism in the outcome?

The women of these chapters convey, each through her own story, insight from the journey. Some are still lost in the valley; some, beginning the climb, see morning rising beyond the rusty slopes. Some of us see only dimly, knowing that what is not seen may be more compelling than what we observe. In the course of the journey we suffer, we learn, we change, we grow. And in the struggles and the stories we give each other, we see etched our own names. We experience pain, grief, joy, triumph, and these we give to each other as well. We "walk through green rooms" of our lives.

> . . . I ascend the moving stairs,
> I descend the moving stairs
> holding in each hand
> the hunger of women
> their songs
> of honey and vinegar

their burdens
of darkness and light.
I walk
through green rooms of my life.

—"Twin Lives"

1

Living Inside

From the time
I was five
I lived inside
Grandfather's house
in the room
next to mine

only a bath
between us
to hold us apart,
his heavy heart
beating stronger
darker than mine.

Living inside
left me hobbled,
I didn't learn
to skip or run,
I didn't learn
to jump or climb,

love to be earned
I thought
meant agreeing
or even being
not visible,
two persons
could live
in the body
at once

but the small I
didn't speak
didn't cry.

I was thirteen
when he died
the house grew
into windows
and doors
I could walk in
I could walk out.

—"Living Inside"

Jane's husband examines her checkbook and criticizes her purchases.

Patricia's fiancé assumes he can use her new red Honda without asking permission.

Jennie's mother reads her journal.

Eileen's father tells her she'll never be a tennis champion like her brother. "She just doesn't have what it takes to be a winner."

Each of these women feels hurt or resentful whenever these situations or similar ones occur. For they are victims of boundary invasions—invasions of the psychological territory that is uniquely their own.

VICTIMS ARE MADE, NOT BORN

Victims of emotional, sexual, or physical abuse often begin to believe that this is a natural way of life. The thinking is that the more we do for others and the more we bear in silence, the less we'll suffer in the long run. We are the little people who seldom provoke an argument or express real feelings; we appear to be content with choices that are made for us by someone else. Why? Because we are still ducking the blows rained on us by an alcoholic father, a dependent mother, or a hostile, domineering husband or brother. If we were to express what we really feel, we might provoke anger, even rage. The dam might break and the turbulent waters rush out and drown us!

What we don't realize is that the dam is already breaking—and it's breaking on our heads. We keep ducking, but the currents seep into our lives and grow higher and higher. There is no safe place to shelter us, and we can't escape the deluge unless we change the course of the stream.

If Jane's husband examines her checkbook, then doesn't he also try to control how she spends her money? And doesn't he begin to point out to her when she is making foolish expenditures—no matter what *his* expenditures may be?

If Patricia allows her fiancé to take her car without ever asking permission, soon he will be charging the gas to her. And once she allows him that liberty, he will think it's fine to take his friends on jaunts when she's not included. Then, if she is still a *good sport* and never protests, she will soon be left behind without either a car or a lover!

If Jennie's mother reads her journal, she probably also listens in on her daughter's telephone conversations, monitors her mail, and barges into her bedroom without knocking.

And it's almost a certainty that Eileen's father doesn't just claim that she'll never be a tennis champion, but implies that she is clumsy, dumb, and will never succeed at anything. He may even wish, volubly, that she had never been born!

Jane, Patricia, Jennie, and Eileen have two options. First, they can remain in the same miserable *stuck* (or unchanging) position in which no matter how much effort or energy they exert, no one is ever pleased. And they are not content either because within these agreeable personas lies a volatile mix of anger, frustration, and repressed hopes, all waiting to explode. These are the narratives of a timid wife who takes a gun and shoots her husband of twenty-five years because he criticizes the way she fried his eggs and of a young woman who cuts off her boyfriend's penis because it symbolizes his violent, aggressive masculinity.

But we can turn to that second option, which poses a risk because it means making changes in our perceptions and behavior. We don't realize that we have choices, choices that were there all along, but we were blind to our feelings of outrage and pain—blinded by the forces of repression and denial unleashed in every unhealthy family system. Once we remove the masks that have closed us off from reality and self-expression, we see for the first time. We see clearly. We can stand up for ourselves, explore new avenues, and say what we feel and think. We can learn to defend ourselves against boundary invasions and any violation of the self.

SIGHTING BOUNDARIES

Each of us recognizes territorial boundaries and how geographical border lines delineate country from country, state from state. And we know immediately when someone intrudes on our physical boundary lines—as when a neighbor dumps grass clippings on our freshly mown lawn, uses our driveway to build an addition to his house, or a robber, forcing a window open, breaks into a bedroom.

Although psychological boundaries are not so readily apparent as geographical borders or physical intrusions, they are just as real because psychological boundaries represent our unique inner territory. In fact, family therapist Salvador Minuchin suggests that boundaries are the key to all human relationships, for they are the emotional barriers that preserve and protect the rights of the individual. If we don't establish clear boundaries in our relationships and a strong sense of identity separate from our parents and family members, we don't grow into emotionally balanced human beings.

THE FAMILY PROCESS:
MURRAY BOWEN'S DEFINITIVE FRAMEWORK

According to family systems theory, the family has a wholeness that is greater than the sum of its parts. In other words, when one individual in the family changes, the whole system shifts. And it may shift with a bang, with every member feeling the repercussions! Past events and experiences combine to produce a series of ongoing circular loops that lead into pathology or addiction. For example, the violent temper of a grandfather may lead to disengagement or separation and withdrawal on the part of the son, and disengagement may be a factor in alcoholism in the next generation. A father's alcoholism may then lead to emotional abusiveness on the part of a son toward his son or daughter, and the cycle continues.

The dynamics that underlie the attitudes and actions of the family system are complex and interlocking, and we need to examine them carefully in our own families to find the pattern and what that configuration means in our lives. Murray Bowen, the theorist and psychotherapist who developed the framework for family systems therapy, believes that family dynamics center around two opposing forces—those that hold us together and those that try to break free to establish independence and individuality. As his concepts form the chief basis for family therapy ideology, it's useful to take a look at them in the context of our own experience and where each of us stands in the continuum from *fusion* (intense attachment) to *differentiation* (or independence).

According to Bowen, when stress between a couple becomes intense, anxiety is relieved by bringing a third person, usually a child, into the relationship. This leads to a heightened bonding or *fusion* between one parent and a child. The triangle is the basic building block of emotional systems, and the family forms a series of interlocking triangles that intermesh in the family process.

The child who is *triangulated* into the relationship becomes the focus of the family emotions such as anger or blame. It's difficult for this child to separate from the parent figure because of the intense *fusion* or *emotional bond,* which may be either angry and conflicting or close and dependent. A *fused* daughter or son will grow up with a low level of differentiation and an inability to separate feeling from thinking.

The *fused* or *undifferentiated* person puts all of her energy into loving or being loved and finds it difficult to differentiate emotion from reason. Responses are determined almost completely by a reactive emotional stance, and there is little attempt to balance feeling with rational thought.

Along the middle of Bowen's scale is the *feeling* person, who has developed a degree of separation from the emotional issues of the parent. She is sensitive to conflict and disharmony, but it's difficult for her to maintain her emotional balance as feelings either soar or plummet at every shift in circumstances.

At the opposite end of the scale from the fused person is the *differentiated* individual, who is able to separate from the emotional issues of the family of origin and who has well-defined opinions and beliefs. The differentiated individual is independent, emotionally balanced, and principle-oriented, and is able to change with changing circumstances. On the other hand, the differentiated person is not unfeeling. She is able to balance emotion and reason, to react with spontaneity and passion, and at the same time, is also capable of restraint.

In the Family Projection Process parents transmit immaturity and dependency (or *lack of differentiation*) to their children. When this happens, we repeat the triangulation process and develop fusion or a lack of boundaries with one child (or more).

The child most involved in the family fusion process, the one who is most intensely attached to a mother or father, will reach a *lower level of differentiation* than her parents, and each succeeding generation will pass on a lower level of maturity or differentiation to the next generation in the Multigenerational Process. Conversely, the child who is least fused with a parent will pass on higher levels of independence and emotional balance—or differentiation—to succeeding generations.

If the individual attempts to resolve overly intense attachments to the family of origin by physical or emotional distancing—in other words, by simply removing herself from the conflicts and entanglements of the family—she experiences *emotional cutoff* and carries unresolved problems with her into any new relationship, and the cycle begins again.

BOUNDARY INVASIONS: A DEFINITION

Although relatively new as a psychological term, boundary invasions are as old as Eve. We deal with these intrusions constantly in our everyday lives—attacks on our self-esteem, our feelings, our sexuality, our bodies; intrusion on our privacy; and attempts to control our lives. Such invasions may be relatively small or, in cases of prolonged physical, sexual, or emotional abuse, may cause serious damage for a lifetime. But whether they are large or small, intrusions on our boundaries are disturbing occurrences, and we have to learn to protect ourselves from the unhappiness they can cause.

As we draw our invisible boundary lines, we are not building walls to keep the enemy out. On the contrary, we keep our lines intact to preserve our relationships! Once we clearly define our boundaries, we begin to communicate openly and directly. And we establish guidelines for what we expect of others—and what we should give them in return. But if we grow up in homes that don't function well in terms of communication or understanding or enter into destructive marriages, boundaries are not respected and we become confused, vulnerable, and insecure. We don't attempt to defend our rights because we don't realize we have any!

The compelling stories told by the women of this study function as a key to understanding how to define boundaries and why this quest is an issue that each of us needs to resolve.

Looking first at Laura's history, we find a dramatic illustration of the trauma, poisonous secrets, and insecurities that spring from the alcoholic family network and the lack of clear boundaries.

LOSING SIGHT OF THE SELF

This is Laura. Light-footed and long-legged, she looks much younger than her almost fifty years. With her dark hair, brown eyes, and expressive face, she could be an Italian countess except for her distinctly southern Alabama accent, red socks, and cotton shorts just above the knees. She is filled with ideas, insights, and plans for the future, and she draws, sculpts, drives her sporty Nissan with apparently unending verve and energy. Laura appears to epitomize vitality and self-confidence.

For more than a decade she held a successful position as vice president of a large commercial realty firm but in the past several years she has decided to devote her energy to the study of fine arts because she has always longed to express herself creatively. Now that her children are grown and she enjoys a fulfilling relationship with her second husband, a man she both loves and admires, she has the time and financial security to explore a whole new realm.

Yet Laura still suffers from feelings of self-doubt and confusion. Beneath the bright, beautiful surface hides a frightened young girl trying desperately to conceal family problems from the community and save her family from certain disgrace. Laura grew up with an alcoholic father, whose moods were volatile and often angry, and a mother who, though loving and caring, was dependent on her children for companionship and affection.

EMOTIONAL ABUSE—ALWAYS AN INVASION!

"I was a lonely little girl," Laura says. "Psychologically, my dad just wasn't there for me or for any of us. When he was home, I did my level best to stay away from him. He could say and do some mean, ornery things, even smashing plates and glasses, whatever came his way. My brothers and I dreaded his coming home after work or after he'd been out drinking with one of his cronies. We knew there might be a terrible scene, with him roaring and my mother crying and trying to appease him or else getting into some obsessive argument she couldn't win. And of course I was my 'mother's daughter,' and he gave up any claim to me early on.

We had few friends. I had a good idea of how my father might be behaving any day of the week, so I seldom invited anyone to come home with me. And I was terribly ashamed of him and how we lived. Of course, since we lived in a small rural town, probably everyone knew."

INVASIONS: HOW DO WE RECOGNIZE THEM?

In her daily meditations book, *The Language of Letting Go*, codependency expert and author Melody Beattie suggests these basic guidelines for recognizing an invasion:

- Who or what don't I trust?
- What doesn't feel right to me?
- What makes me unhappy or resentful?
- What makes me angry or sad?
- What makes me uncomfortable or shames me?

Once we answer questions like these honestly, we begin to define the intrusions that upset us. And we recognize an invasion immediately if we listen to the small voice that connects us with our very real feelings of sorrow or pain or frustration. That voice has a way of speaking out clearly. It may whisper, "I feel sad . . . or lonely . . . or guilty" or shout, "That makes me mad!" or scream, "Ouch, that hurts!" But this voice takes no prompting and no translation. It means what it says!

INVASIONS IN THE ALCOHOLIC FAMILY SYSTEM

"I didn't have a lot of privacy ever," Laura says softly. "For one thing, until my brothers left, I shared a room with Mother. Dad was banished to his small kingdom in the back. Probably he preferred it that way so he could come and go as he pleased. I can't imagine that my parents had much of a sex life, if any, although things may have been better before all of us (myself and my two brothers) came along and Dad's drinking accelerated to the point that he had no real relationship with anyone.

Once I remember he broke into my little piggy bank and took money I had been saving for a sweater. I still think that was the lowest of the low. He probably went out and bought a quart of whiskey with it.

You have to realize there wasn't much help for drinkers back then. AA was just getting started, and it wasn't around, at least not in a small backwater town in Alabama. My father went to a mental hospital once just to dry out. That's all they knew back then, get them sober and hope for the best.

My two brothers left home as soon as they could. Now that I look back on it, my father wasn't all bad. He did his best to provide for us. But he was far gone in his addiction and a heavy daily drinker. When he was drinking, he was abusive, scary. I knew I had to get Mother out of that household before I went off to business school.

With a lot of pushing from me, she finally left. At age forty-five she went to work as a waitress. You can imagine how hard that was, but she did it. A year later my father was dead, killed in an accident involving drinking. I still don't know all the details. Nobody wanted to talk about it, including me.

Now that I've been down the same route myself and am a recovering alcoholic, I have a little more sympathy for my father and what was going on. But I was never like him, never abusive or violent or out of control with my emotions. Yet I had a problem stopping after one or two drinks. That scared the life out of me. I had seen all too clearly how quickly everything goes down the drain once alcohol kicks in. I decided to give up drinking and start going to AA. My husband and I did it together, and I've never regretted it. But that's getting ahead of my story."

THE LONELY CONFIDANTE

"From the time I can remember I was Mother's unspoken ally. She had no best friend—I was it!" Laura relates. "She told me almost everything, and the more I knew, the more I disliked my father. What she told me I think was pretty much true, but what I didn't understand as a child was that her descriptions were colored by the fury of her emotions. She was caught in a situation where she felt absolutely helpless.

Since I had no close friends while growing up, Mother had an effective technique for keeping me in line. Whenever I didn't live up to her expectations, she would remind me that she was 'the best friend I had,' and then withdraw her affection until I shaped up. She was playing games with me all the time, but neither of us realized what she was doing.

Mother was no respecter of privacy either. I suspect she was snoopy and read the journal that I kept. This was her way of protecting me, but her protection left me feeling vulnerable and afraid. There was nothing I could hide from her."

Even as she speaks, it's clear that Laura feels the emotional intensity of her early relationship with her mother. "Mother was so afraid for me," she reflects. "Once when I was about fifteen, I was going into town with a friend to the drugstore, and I was dressed 'scantily' (her term) in shorts and a cotton bra-type halter. She went absolutely berserk, ranting and raving like a demented person. I was already well-endowed even then, and I think my emerging sexuality enraged and frightened her. She was certain I'd turn into a 'loose woman.' Feminine sexuality must have been terribly threatening to her. You can understand it when you realize she had been tyrannized by her gender and her powerless position as a woman.

Back in those days, the sixties, women usually didn't work outside the home, and Mother wasn't equipped for it anyway. She had only a high school education, and the only job she could get was as a clerk in a store, with long, exhausting hours and a minuscule paycheck. She was stuck, and she knew it."

CODEPENDENCY: WHAT DOES IT MEAN?

We might think of Laura's mother as *codependent,* the term used to connote an individual caught in an abusive situation who has become both victim and enabler. But is a woman codependent because she stays in an unhealthy relationship? The question is: does she stay because of inner feelings of inadequacy and low self-esteem, believing that she can only be valued in relationships where she is taking care of others, or does she stay because of viable life concerns?

In dealing with codependency, we may underestimate the importance of outside forces such as financial dependency and concerns for children. After all, in our society the children belong to the woman—the money to the man! Sixty-nine percent of single family homes, with the mother as sole support, live on less than $20,000 a year and many on much less. Some 80 percent of these single mothers have only a high school education (or less), so their prospects for climbing out of poverty and their straitened circumstances are extremely limited. We have to take a good look, then, at the hard terms of economic survival before we condemn a woman who chooses to stay with an abusive or exploitative mate. In addition, the woman may fear for her life and safety and for the safety of her children if she tries to leave or even to change her mate's behavior.

Although the options are becoming greater for women who suffer violence at the hands of an abuser, there still are not enough shelters or social service agencies to go around. Sometimes there is a waiting list of days or weeks. And there are men who track down their wives wherever they go and make life for them and their children an unmitigated hell. For women with few outside resources and support systems, the possibilities appear meager indeed.

The current concept of codependency agrees with family systems thinking in that it emphasizes the circularity of behavior, that the family is affected by the behavior of each member. When one member plays the pathological or alcoholic role, the spouse takes up the corresponding role of rescuer and enabler. And codependency theory recognizes, as does family systems thinking, that it's important for the woman to set limits in her relationships and refuse to tolerate abusive behavior of the alcoholic or addict. However, at this juncture the two points of view diverge.

A growing number of practicing psychologists suggests that women stuck in these situations are not sick or diseased but are simply part of the complex interworking of the family system. It's natural for women to want to help a troubled family member or friend. Problems arise only when the woman becomes too focused on someone else's issues and underfocused on her own. Current codependency theory appears to attribute too much blame to the rescuer and too little to the alcoholic or sick person who suffers from a "progressive disease." If we carry codependency thinking to the extreme, we blame the victim and exonerate the perpetrator because he is suffering from a "disease." On the other hand, AA theory clearly states that *each individual is responsible for his or her own behavior,* no matter what damage he or she may have suffered in the past.

My own view is that the codependent individual is almost identical to Bowen's undifferentiated person. We are *codependent*—or *undifferentiated*—when we look to another person to fulfill our basic psychological needs. If we are dependent on a spouse or a loved one to solve our problems, take care of our responsibilities, or provide the force and direction for our lives, then we are codependent. If we expect a marital partner or a lover to build our self esteem, then we are certain to be disappointed because no one can do that for us. And no amount of reassurance can give us what we are looking for—the confidence that we are capable, talented, skilled, intelligent, and lovable, that we can manage our own lives.

Codependents can't make decisions for themselves; they are baffled and troubled when they have to make choices. They don't trust their own judgment or their own resources. They are dependent on other people to fill in the voids, whatever they may be. Laura's mother illustrates a number of the symptoms of codependency—the drawing of her daughter into the marital conflict, the dependency on Laura, a child, to alleviate her loneliness and despair. But looking at the situation in context, we realize that Laura's mother was also trapped within the confines of her marriage, both economically and socially, with no skills or education to permit her escape until her children were grown and self-supporting.

COALITIONS: FORMING AN ALLIANCE AGAINST THE ENEMY

In the alcoholic family a tremendous amount of energy goes down the drain. All of the family's efforts are focused on the alcoholic's behavior and trying to control it. The family task is twofold—trying to restrain the addict from drinking and hiding the family's shameful secret from the community. But of course both of these are hopeless tasks because we can't control anyone's behavior but our own. And we can't hide the drinker in the closet or under the bed because he's always bounding out again when we least expect it. Almost certainly, wherever he is, he is causing chaos. Of course the chaos at home is the most explosive since family members are standing close by. It's as if you stood in the eye of the storm and asked hurricane-force winds to stop blowing!

The unpredictable, violent, frightening father was the center of the storm in Laura's family and no amount of pleading and prayers could create a semblance of peace. Laura and her brothers, instead of receiving reassurance and support from their parents, stepped up into an adult role and were the caretakers—in charge of protecting Mother from the forces that threatened to destroy them all. Laura became the family hero (or heroine), mowing the lawn when it was overgrown with weeds and grass, running errands, making good grades in school. Somehow if Laura were smart and brave enough, the family would miraculously be saved.

There's another interesting phenomenon in Laura's family system—*coalitions in the making!* A coalition forms when a mother or father takes sides with a child, drawing the son or daughter into an unhappy alliance against the other partner. Often, as in Laura's case, the mother will pull her children into an alliance against a detached and hostile father. Laura and her brothers felt forced to stand with their mother, defend and take care of her, leaving the father a distant member looking in from the outside. Every family member was entwined in an angry conflict he or she couldn't resolve. And the more isolated the father became, the more he withdrew in anger and confusion, cut off from both society and the family.

INVASIONS: LAURA'S LONG LIST

Let's look at the *boundary invasions* Laura was subjected to. First, there was physical violence in the home. Her father smashed and broke things in fits of irrational alcoholic temper. He was progressively emotionally abusive as the drinking heightened. There was blaming and taunting on the part of both parents, with terrible scenes between them, Father screaming and Mother crying in the background.

Her mother, on the other hand, was intrusive and wanted desperately to control her children's lives. She pried into Laura's private emotional life, reading her letters and journals, searching through her drawers for secrets. Because she was terribly fearful for her children, she tried to tell them how to dress, how to act, and which friends they should choose. This was especially for true for Laura, the only daughter. Mother was strict and demanding, yet treated Laura as a confidante and companion, robbing her of the pleasures and freedom of childhood. It isn't surprising that Laura had very little sense of her own identity.

Laura had little opportunity to learn any *respect for individual boundaries*. Hers were constantly under fire. Her father stole from her bank; she "roomed" with her mother who, at one moment, shared every emotional upheaval with her, and at another, reacted with rage and dismay as Laura threatened to grow up and become a woman with her own personality and sexual identity.

DEPENDENCY AND ISOLATION: THE FAMILY LEGACY

Laura's family, greatly shamed by the abusive, alcoholic father, developed *rigid external boundaries* that cut them off almost entirely from the outside world, the church, school, and community. Laura and her brothers had few friends while growing up, and Laura was her mother's "best and only friend." Laura didn't dare bring classmates home because she never knew if her father would arrive home drunk and quarrelsome or if her parents would be engaged in a loud argument. She was embarrassed at the way her home looked—the furniture shabby, the rugs worn and faded, the lawn overgrown. Both shamed and frightened by her father's violent behavior, she also felt the tension of her erratic relationship with her mother.

Yet there is a dichotomy here: the more miserable and shamed the family becomes, the more members cling to each other for love, companionship, and all ordinary activities and the more enmeshed and dependent they become. The division between the generation blurs; a daughter becomes a "sister," "a little mother," a son becomes the "little man" of the house. A twisted vine of suffering and dependency grows up around them, choking off communication with others, shutting out the light around them. No one knows where to turn!

With Laura and her mother, we see a classic example of *weak boundaries* or *fusion*. With weak or fused boundaries, there's no line between the roles of children and those of parents in the family hierarchy. And there's no distinction between the generations. We are adults one minute, children the next. Laura was Mother's friend, companion, life support, housekeeper, and daughter! On Monday she was her mother's confidante, on Friday, a child again, reproved and sent to bed early when she tried to assert her feelings. However, boundary divisions vary between family members, and boundary lines between Laura's father and mother and between the father and children were rigid and distant, allowing for little communication or affection.

Laura's life was bound up so tightly in a *fused* filial relationship that she could barely separate her own identity from that of her mother. Her emotions were so shaped by those of her mother that it became almost impossible in adolescence for her to break away and begin the task of building self-confidence and independence. Mother's needs were overwhelming, much more than a daughter could hope to satisfy, leaving Laura in a constant state of anxiety and confusion.

In fact, just as Laura in her early teens was beginning to feel comfortable in her role as her mother's companion, the situation reversed itself, and Mother wanted to turn back the clock and make her a child again. Was Laura really being provocative when she wore a revealing halter top or was this a natural response for a budding adolescent? She had no one to turn to for guidance or understanding, and again was stuck in the old groove of helplessness and frustration. Being stuck in psychological terms simply means that we resist change and remain fixed in the familiar negative patterns set by the family rules.

CONFUSING MESSAGES

Laura looks puzzled and sad even now as she says, "I think one of my big problems during my childhood, aside from the chaotic scene at home, was Mother's ambivalent message, 'You can do anything,' and in the next breath, 'You're just like me. You'll never succeed.' The variation on that theme was, 'If you fail, it's not surprising because you're nervous and you take after me.' There are things I know I could have done—singing, painting, drawing, playing the piano—but the horror was always there. I might fail. I shouldn't even try since I was just like Mother, and look at her!"

Mother's advice to Laura is another *boundary invasion* because contradictory messages like this constitute a subtle form of emotional abuse. In the guise of loving care, Laura's mother was gradually undermining her daughter's sense of self, a basic faith that could have given her the strength to take risks, even small ones. To add to Laura's confusion, Mother's messages were impossible to decipher since the two statements, each delivered with a freighted emotional intensity, were the direct opposite of each other—"yes, you are wonderful . . . you can do anything" followed by an emphatic "no, you can't . . . don't even try."

Pain and disappointment are part of the learning process, and when Laura's mother deprived her daughter of the risk of failure, she also deprived her of the opportunity to succeed. Even if Laura didn't succeed, at least she would learn in the process and begin again. Although Laura didn't attempt to draw or play the piano, ironically she was left with the conviction that she was a failure. She was afraid even to try! Fortunately, Laura today has overcome many of her childhood insecurities and is deeply involved in learning photography, history, music, and painting—all of the creative ventures she missed as a child.

Laura says, "I grew up being afraid. Afraid of myself, my energy, sex, drive, vitality. All of these qualities, which are basically *me*, got me into trouble at school and at home. I wouldn't know until later how narrow and limited my life had been. The very qualities that are my strengths now were my undoing then."

REPEATING FAMILIAR PATTERNS

"When I finished high school, I didn't know what to do next, so I went to business school and finished in half the allotted time," Laura states. "I then had to get a job. I was only eighteen years old and had no idea what direction my life should take. I took the easy (or so I thought) alternative. I married Johnny and had three children. Because I was unsure of myself I fenced myself into the Super Woman role. I had to do everything, be all things to everyone. And Johnny fenced me into an even smaller space—he couldn't stand for me to be strong and successful. This absolutely undid him. But at that point nobody encouraged me to think I was worthwhile, and I had to keep proving that I was to myself.

I began to have a purpose and a reason for stretching and redefining myself when I had my three children. They were the first things that were worth fighting for. I had to make some tough choices then, both for myself and for them, and in making those choices, I changed. I took a first step toward becoming myself, and after a seventeen-year marriage, I left John. I still didn't know what I wanted to do! But I pulled up stakes and went to a city where I didn't know a soul. I knew I had to.

Of course I didn't choose the right job that first time around. They had so little respect for me in that organization that when a wino came in one day and threatened me with a knife, my boss made light of the incident. I had talked this crazed man out of using a knife on me, and my supervisor thought it was a joke! I got out of there fast and went on to a series of less than challenging secretarial jobs until I found a good company where I worked for years. I had a lot of maturity by then.

I think in that interim period of growing up and beginning to find out who I was, I suffered a form of sexual 'misuse.' When a situation came along in which a man tried to force intimacy on me, I was sometimes struck dumb instead of being enraged. I didn't know enough to defend myself! It was surprising for someone as strong and verbal as I am. I think the rationale was that I didn't want to hurt anyone. *My* feelings are what I should have been concerned about, but I didn't know that. I didn't know I was that important. I would like to have been spared that experience—that needless descent in my scale of self-worth.

I finally reached the point, though, that I thought, 'I don't need any of you.' What a liberation that was, that I could pick and choose and speak out. When I met Will, I was ready. I spoke out early on all those man-woman issues and he respected me for it. I more or less said, 'Hold on—I have a few things I want to tell you!' I did finally learn, and the great part is I learned in time."

Laura had finally begun to listen to the inner voice, and not only to listen, but to hear exactly what it said. In the past, out of fear and insecurity, she had tried to close off thoughts that kept her in touch with her instinctive feelings. She had been brought up to believe that you can't trust feelings. Terrible things might happen if you express anger or outrage—the hurricane may sweep you up and blow you away! Like many of us, she was used to rationalizing: *he didn't mean it . . . he had a bad day . . . I don't really care.*

The truth is she did care. And *we* care. We care a great deal. When we forget to listen to ourselves, we not only repress that one experience, we repress all our feelings of pain and fear and anger. We begin to lose touch, just as Laura did, with the real self that defines us and gives us power over our lives.

OUTGROWING DEPENDENCY

"I have always had a terrible fear of my mother dying," Laura relates. "In spite of our complicated and sometimes difficult relationship, I didn't know whether I could withstand the emotional loss—maybe because so many feelings had never been resolved between us. Last year when we were in Seattle, I got a call saying Mother had had a heart attack, and I rushed to Mobile to her hospital bed. I told her how sad I had been when I left home at eighteen, and she said, 'I never knew.' She also told me, 'You were a gift to me.' I had waited all my life to hear that! I knew I was loved, but I had never thought it was unconditional.

Mother's heart attack has opened up the most wonderful years of our relationship. Now she allows me to bathe her and care for her when I go down to see her, and she talks about death and dying with curiosity and interest, not self-pity. She knows now that she was wrong in her attitudes, that she was too hard on us while we were growing up. But she had a difficult life; she didn't know anything else.

When I go down to see her now, we plan little outings. I took her to Gulfport last week and to a museum. She was exposed to paintings and sculpture for the first time in her life. I can let her go now because she knows her death may be soon and accepts it and because we have been able to talk everything out between us honestly and with love and understanding."

THE FAMILY PROCESS AT WORK

Laura's alcoholic family system illustrates the workings of Bowen's concept of family dynamics. First we find *triangulation*—the process by which a parent takes the focus off her own conflicts and projects feelings of anxiety onto a child. Laura was the chief bearer of the family burdens, and she was drawn into a *fused relationship* with her mother, a relationship of dependency, frustration, and isolation. As a young woman, she was pulled into the *family projection process,* forming a first marriage that was a repetition in many ways of her parents' alliance—a confused marital relationship in which Laura would attempt to resolve dependency issues inherent in her intense childhood attachment to her mother. Although it was difficult and painful, Laura would gradually move away from the pathological patterns of the family and free herself and her children from the dark ethos of the *multigenerational process.* As her narrative moves forward, we discover how Laura grows and changes, builds a strong sense of self, and gradually breaks the chain of pathology.

BOUNDARY NEGOTIATIONS

Minuchin proposes that when a couple marries, they need to immediately begin the process of *accommodation* and *boundary making.* The first priority is to work out major issues—such as where they will live and if they will have children. Then they need to resolve minor issues—the practical details of everyday living, who will do the shopping, the cooking, the cleaning, schedules as to when they will watch television or go to bed. If the union is to be a healthy one, each person must adjust to the other's wants and expectations and must be flexible enough to change to accommodate the marital partner. The couple must be willing to negotiate their individual boundaries as well as those that separate them from the outside community.

Since each person comes from a family with varying degrees of *enmeshment* (or attachment) and *disengagement* (or separation), each will be most comfortable with the degree of closeness or separation they have known in the family of origin. Expectations will probably differ dramatically, depending on the background of family interrelationships. This process of boundary negotiation is the most difficult to resolve. A husband's major focus may be on his career and ambitions; a wife's may be on bringing up the children. He may want to distance himself in order to travel or to concentrate on building a successful business; she wants to draw closer bonds between them as her own career is sublimated to his. Each believes that the other spouse is demanding, unreasonable, and selfish.

When a child enters the picture, the family paradigm grows even more complex, bringing greater stress to bear on the marriage. Boundary lines have to be renegotiated to fit the transformation in the pattern. The woman will usually be called on to make drastic alterations at every phase of her life, and she will need greater support from her husband. He, in turn, may resent her demands as intrusive and unreasonable.

When the marital partners are able to accommodate to changing circumstances and adapt interpersonal boundaries to fit new modes, then a healthy, flexible relationship evolves. When the family stays in the old molds in spite of changing situations and events, they increase the rigidity of the structure and trouble is in the making!

BOUNDARY NEGOTIATION AND CONTROL

Even now with a fulfilling second marriage, Laura finds the old issue of control—making decisions, self-expression—rearing its dark head!

"We have a wonderful marriage," Laura says thoughtfully. "Will encourages me in my artistic pursuits, and he doesn't stint when it comes to clothes for me or my art. He is most generous in anything neutral. He believes I am deserving, and he likes to see me expand and grow. That is his great gift, I think.

But that's not to say we don't have our problems and arguments. When we were building our new house in the country, it was almost our undoing. This house was his dream, and he didn't have space for my ideas. My wishes were terribly threatening to him, so in the beginning I gave up and said, 'You can have all of this'—everything to do with planning and building the house. And I didn't do anything for a year. I didn't even look at a magazine.

What he wanted then was a 'yes' person. When we were finished, I felt helpless and lost because he held the cards. He held the check-book!

Even as strong women, we get 'cut off at the knees,' don't we? We are simply powerless because in most cases, especially for our genera-tion, the man makes the money. To give Will credit, I think he feels a terrible conflict over this. And yet a kind of terror takes over with him when it comes to making the big decisions about money. He is finally aware of it and is learning to deal with it. And of course it isn't money—it's control! When I tried to assert myself and say what I wanted, espe-cially when it came to the house, he saw it as a woman being contrary, a woman who wants her own way, a woman out of control!

We were trying to operate *without any boundaries*. It was an under-stood—he had no use for them. He had fixed ideas about how he wanted to spend his time and his money. Now I had spent several years on my own (between the two marriages), making all of my own decisions. And he made all the decisions in his first marriage. We both came to realize that neither of us wanted the other telling us what to do.

What he was afraid of basically was standing there and having to deal with me as an equal with an equal say. Now we have worked out a kind of compromise that still is not without its rough edges—the art is mine and half the house, the landscaping and the other half-house are Will's. Which half? We're still not absolutely sure. But now we are able to put boundaries in there."

TAKING RISKS

Laura's life has never been simple or smooth, but if we look at the emerging pattern, we see her growing and changing, throwing off the old bonds of dependency, gradually realizing her own talents and strengths. In her first marriage Laura was still playing the role of the *good daughter,* the obedient wife, and mother. But she slowly began to realize that she couldn't live with this kind of repression. Building a growing sense of purpose through her children, she was willing to take risks and step out of the tattered robes that she had long ago outgrown.

When Laura struck out and left the safety and the confines of her marriage, this was a tremendous act of courage, a daring step. Al-though her situation was difficult in the first few years after the divorce, she was building confidence in her capabilities in the workplace and in her sense of herself as an attractive, talented woman.

It was also necessary for Laura to shake off the old feelings of dependency on her mother, an ambivalent relationship fraught with both pain and tenderness. She couldn't abandon her mother, leaving her without love or support, but gradually she began to establish firmer boundary lines, refusing to be pulled back into the old emotional intensity of anger, bitterness, and loneliness. It wasn't until her mother's heart attack and convalescence, however, that Laura could speak out honestly and begin to resolve the old feelings of guilt and dependency.

Laura is still working out tangled issues of control and power with her husband, Will. Despite the ties of love and respect that hold the marriage close, Laura has had to learn the delicate act of balancing love with the need for self-expression. She and Will are both strong personalities with definite ideas about what they want for themselves. Will encourages Laura to study, reflect, and spend much of her time painting, reading, and sculpting. But he sees their home as a fulfillment of all his dreams, and it's difficult, almost impossible, for him to let any fraction of that dream go. At the same time, Laura realizes that she must have a voice in all the issues between them, including the creation of their home. That voice won't be stilled any longer!

Is control a boundary issue? It certainly is! Whenever another person—father, mother, husband, or friend—tries to control our lives by telling us what to think, how to behave, what to spend and how, these are distinct boundary invasions. Keep a close watch.

DEFINE YOUR BOUNDARIES

Laura gradually learned that, for the sake of her own survival and that of her children, she had to make changes in her life. And with the help of counseling, study, and reflection, her own inherently strong personality has emerged. But Laura contends she couldn't have reached this point without the guidance of a counselor plus the firm and loving support of AA groups and the twelve-step framework for living a full life.

Laura still experiences periods of self-doubt and ambivalence, yet is now strong enough to confront the conflicts that have haunted her since childhood. Her creative life, too, is in full bloom, with hours devoted to sculpting, drawing, and painting, along with nurturing her inner spiritual life.

These are the steps that work for Laura:

1. Break away from family constricts and negative patterns.
2. Believe in yourself—that you are a worthwhile person who deserves respect—and build on your strengths.
3. Take risks—fight for what is important to you.
4. Set limits in relationships and communicate your feelings and needs. Be honest and direct, but never cruel.
5. Commit to the support and framework of a twelve-step self-help program.

As Laura says so compellingly, "This business of being a woman is a very complex and intricate thing. We are just starting to look at it in our society. You can go for a long time and not realize what has been holding you down. Every generation of daughters is born, I think, into a more enlightened age.

I believe that I myself am a handful! A lot of assertiveness and contrariness and talents that come with the personality—the ying and the yang of it. I do realize that it takes a strong person to deal with me.

But I like that. I like a person who is willing to tangle with me and speak his piece and then work it all out. I like Will's intelligence, his groundedness, his sense of humor. Now we are able to put boundaries in our conflicts. They are new to Will—this sense of setting limits—but at the same time they are familiar. That we are working at our problems all the time shows we're not going to stay stuck with them. It shows how much we care!"

THE GENDER TRAP

Even when we grow up in healthy families where there is support, communication, and respect, there is another trap that we as women have to learn to avoid. I call this the *gender trap.*

What do I mean by the gender trap? Simply that women continue to have serious problems setting boundaries during the course of their everyday lives. Men, too, have their share of boundary conflicts and feelings of dependency. Any boy who has grown up in a neglectful or abusive home is not likely to have a clear sense of his own identity or to respect the boundaries of others as he grows into manhood. And it is equally important for men to recognize and defend their boundaries in establishing healthy relationships.

Yet women, historically, have held positions of diminished power in our society, and in spite of tremendous sociological changes in the latter part of the twentieth century, we continue to feel that we are being selfish—women out of control—when we demand rights and privileges for ourselves. Just last week I asked a spirited older woman why she had stayed in a hostile and loveless marriage for over thirty years and why she had continued to live within the confines of that abusive relationship year after year. Her answer: "I didn't know I had a choice."

Our feelings of self-doubt are not surprising when we remember that up until the time of the Industrial Revolution in the nineteenth century, women were regarded as inferior—intellectually, emotionally, and physically. We were not considered qualified for higher education, were not allowed to own property in our own name, and could not even make decisions, in most cases, concerning our children's discipline, education, and marriages.

The women's movement, begun in 1848 in America, was championed by such stalwarts as Elizabeth Cady Stanton and Lucretia Mott, who led the fight for women's rights to own property, attain an education, be paid a fair wage, and vote. It was an uphill battle, with women being mocked, jailed, force-fed, and reviled, and it was not until 1920 in this country that the women's suffrage movement won out, and women finally began to vote!

Gradually, women were reluctantly granted equality under the law, an opportunity to be educated, to own property separately from a spouse, and to enter all professions and trades. But, as we are all well aware, there is still a stigma attached to outspoken expressions of women like Gloria Steinem or Hillary Clinton, who are denounced as "unfeminine," "arrogant," or "aggressive." And women who enter male-dominated professions such as engineering, carpentry, and plumbing are still subjected to overt suspicion and hostility.

Despite tremendous strides women have achieved over the past three decades, it's difficult for many of us to recognize what our rights are in all of our relationships. We don't know because we, as mothers, daughters, sisters, and wives, have been trained since childhood to be giving, submissive, and patient. We have been taught, subtly yet clearly, that a woman's role, whether she is a homemaker or a corporate lawyer, is to sublimate her own needs to those of her family and society.

To sort out who we are as women and as individuals, and to decide what we want for ourselves, we have to begin at the beginning with the attachment process between parent and child. For once we become parents, we introduce immense challenges and complexities into our lives, and these are not always easily resolved.

> The lake blooms, contains me,
> bears my summers like flowers
> that burn through the sand.
> *Why do you stand*
> the lake wonders
> *shifting light into shadow,*
> *shadow to sun.*
> The trails know my story.
> Ask them.
>
> —"The Old Rail Trail"

2

Pastures of Clover

Edges. Her grandfather taught her
about edges, the deep
secret borders of rooms,
tall kitchen stools
where a child's legs dangled,
missing a rung.
He shouted move slowly,
not making a sound,
don't sing in your sleep,
your song is too quick and too loud . . .

But her voice grew rose edges,
petals bled on the rug,
leaving soft stains
he crushed when he closed
out the lights,
scrubbed his hands clean.
His bay belly trembled,
his vest pocket watch

keeping good time
he heaped his plate full,
syrup and biscuits,
sausage and eggs, eggs
swimming loose from the shell.
His gold pocket watch keeping
strict time, he spoke sweetly
of Heaven and Hell.
He hated stray petals, especially
red petals, the color of clover,

the color of blood.
Hydrangeas blinded him,
blue of her eyes.
He closed all the windows,
shuttered the shades,
but at each door sprang blue blossoms
and pastures of clover,
red crimson clover
she saw as she woke when he died.

—"Pastures of Clover"

Ellen is a petite, vivacious woman, now in her early seventies. She loves music, theater, art, and poetry. Wearing matching shoes, sweaters, and scarves, bright coral or purple, she is a natural performer who will recite a poem or an anecdote before a large, noisy audience without a trace of self-consciousness. Ellen also is a woman of many talents who has studied piano, painting, drawing, and literature, and is a writer of poetry and plays. And she is never at a loss for words—either spoken or written.

But Ellen endured a painful lonely childhood that took time, intensive therapy, and the backing of friends and support groups over the years to overcome. She has had to struggle with escalating feelings of anxiety because of missing links in the relationship with a cold, hostile mother and a distant, detached father.

A TWISTED TALE

"Mother's family was definitely male-oriented," Ellen says, her words tumbling out quickly. "My grandmother died when Mother was only six, and from that time on she believed (unconsciously of course) that women can't be trusted. They abandon you. They die. Mother's father, my English grandfather, became the 'sun, moon, and stars' to his children. My grandparents were stern, dour Britishers, born in England, although my mother was born here. They believed that life was hard and painful from birth to death, and because they thought that, that's what it was for them and for my mother. All gloom and doom.

I grew up as an only child. I didn't think I was pretty or smart or lovable in any way. My parents were disappointed in me, in each other, and, I suppose, in just about everything. Of course I didn't realize why as a child and that they had created their own unhappiness. I just thought there was something wrong with me and I was to blame for all our misery. It was a lot for a little girl to carry around. I was naturally small, and I wanted to shrink into being totally invisible so that no one could blame me or shout at me or even see me!

Mother never took the time to teach me anything. She was impatient, and I was much too slow. She would have me stand on a stool and would dress me completely until I was quite old, probably eleven or twelve. I remember vividly my mother's friend coming by, and when she saw this tableau of my mother dressing me, she was shocked. 'Aren't you ashamed, a big girl like you?' she asked.

I was humiliated. I didn't realize (even at that age) that I should be doing for myself because Mother wouldn't let me. She completely took over, and the whole ordeal of tying my shoes and buttoning my blouse would be painful because Mother didn't pretend to enjoy my company. I don't think she even liked me!

It wouldn't have been so bad if she had simply disliked me and was willing to leave me alone. But she watched me all the time. She would trample on me in the kitchen if I tried to help, step on my heels or elbow me. She wanted to do it all herself and at the same time she hated the drudgery. But she had to have that kind of power—that only *she* could bake the perfect cake or make up the proper bed."

ANOTHER UNIVERSE OPENS UP

"It never occurred to me that I could make it on my own! Mother didn't think I was capable of putting a piece of toast in the oven, and I assumed she was right. Fortunately, at eighteen, I won a full scholarship to the New York School of Design. I began to make friends and to enter the world, the museums, the shops, the foreign films. I loved it! When I finished school, I found a job in the city, and I could window-shop by the hour. But even though I was miserable and felt unloved and unwanted by my parents, I lived at home until I was thirty-seven years old and married for the first time. I didn't know anything else.

Although I went home to my parents every night (an hour and a half commute), I fooled myself into thinking that I was living my own life. But I wasn't. I wasn't called on to be responsible for myself, get my meals, clean up, make my own decisions. Yet I disliked my loveless home, where there was no affection from anyone and nothing was ever any fun. We didn't even have a dog!"

DRAWING THE INVISIBLE LINES BETWEEN US

With Ellen (as with Laura) we find a classic example of *weak boundary lines* between mother and daughter. If our boundaries are weak, we don't respect or defend our inner selves. We don't know how because we don't know what our rights or roles are! We never stop trying to please others. We become victims because we allow others to take advantage of us and never understand why we feel bitter or resentful. And yet (although it's hard to realize), no one can take advantage of us unless we allow it.

According to family systems thinking, we have varying boundary lines in all our relationships that are *weak, rigid,* or *flexible*:

Figure 2.1
Diagram of Boundary Lines

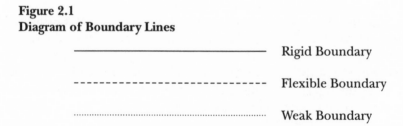

At the other end of the scale, *rigid boundary lines* develop. As the term suggests, rigid boundary lines mean rigid rules. Laws are made by one parent or the other—often the father figure—and we can't deviate from them. With rigid boundaries we tend to isolate ourselves, to become as detached as we possibly can so we won't feel anything. We don't communicate and we don't let anyone get close to us. We might get hurt!

In contrast, in the healthy family, members have *flexible boundaries that are resilient but strong*. Ideally, the family is a connecting unit, each member supporting the other, with three or four generations interacting and communicating. Members have a clear sense of individual rights and responsibilities and the freedom to express feelings and opinions as well as to make choices. Since boundaries are flexible, they are constantly changing and adapting, particularly at times of life-altering crises such as birth, death, marriage, illness, or a job loss or promotion.

Healthy family development takes place when boundaries between family members are clearly delineated, anxiety is relatively low, and individuals maintain good contact with the family of origin. But when contact with the family of origin produces anxiety and conflict, we don't maintain close connections. The boundaries separating us from the nuclear family then become rigid, allowing little interplay between us and our siblings or parents. And when contact lapses, we are apt to forget the pain and discord of the relationships. We experience *emotional cutoff* without ever resolving our ambivalent feelings, and we carry these feelings of bitterness or anger or pain into our current intimate relationships.

TESTING THE FAMILY STRUCTURE

Minuchin envisions a family continuum that marks our movement from *enmeshment* (or overly intense attachment) to *disengagement* (or rigid separation) from the family of origin. *Enmeshment* simply means that we have weak boundaries and are highly dependent on the feelings and ideas of a parent to determine our own ideas and feelings. Closely enmeshed families have relatively closed *external boundaries,* and members are not expected to find close relationships outside the family circle. Growth and change in such families are seen as disloyalty and betrayal and experienced as an actual loss of self.

In *disengaged* families, with rigid boundaries, there is little support or affection, and family members scarcely seem to be aware of each other's feelings or ideas. There is little communication between them, and the emphasis is on industry, independence, and achievement rather than any close bonding.

Is your family enmeshed or disengaged—or somewhere in the middle? The following are simple criteria for making that decision:

Enmeshed Systems:
1. Does one family member often speak for all the others?
2. Is one parent highly concerned about all activities and problems of the child or several children?
3. Does the family restrict differences of opinion?
4. Are most opinions and experiences shared?

Disengaged Systems:

1. Do members seem indifferent or insensitive to one another?
2. Does a parent (or both parents) try to block communications from children or other relatives?
3. Do family members avoid close physical contact?
4. Is there little affect or energy passing between brothers and sisters, children and parents, husband and wife?

DEPENDENCY AND WEAK BOUNDARIES GO HAND IN HAND

When asked why she didn't rebel against her mother's dictates and get a place of her own once she could afford it, Ellen recalls simply that she was afraid. Because her mother had dominated her life for so long, fostering a deceptive chain of dependency, guilt, and help-lessness, she never felt she was a separate person entitled to a fulfill-ing separate life or that she was capable of making a decision on her own. And at the same time, Mother showed little affection or sup-port. Ellen experienced the worst of both worlds!

"One of my strongest memories is of trying to hide everything I felt," Ellen says. "Even when I didn't say anything, somehow Mother knew. I became a deceitful person out of sheer desperation, trying to achieve some kind of privacy and to avoid my mother's attention, which was sure to be negative. I was never allowed to express my real feelings. I was slowly suffocating and wondered why I couldn't breathe."

Ellen's family pattern was a tangled web of deceit and denial, where Ellen always appeared to be at fault. The real source of the mother's resentment, Ellen would learn much later, was her unexpected preg-nancy at eighteen and the forced marriage to Ellen's father, a man her mother didn't love. So Ellen had caused all the trouble simply by being born! In her mother's eyes an unwanted daughter—this clumsy child who could never learn—had interrupted her chance for a ca-reer and tied her to the house for a lifetime!

At the same time the mother fostered the very traits of dependency and insecurity in Ellen that might have enabled her to escape. Be-cause her mother always had to be in control, she forced Ellen into the same helpless mold she pretended to despise.

"And all the while this was going on," Ellen reiterates, "I could never say what I thought or felt. I could never express the very real pain that was at the center of my childhood because if I did, Mother might have to take a look at her own. And since I wasn't taught skills, never praised for what I did achieve, and, in contrast, criticized and blamed for whatever happened, I found it impossible to believe that I could be a person of any talent or competence."

THE ATTACHMENT PROCESS STARTS EARLY

Child psychoanalyst, Margaret Mahler, discovered in her work with emotionally disturbed children that if the mother or caretaker fails to give the child warmth and affection during the first critical months of life, the baby may feel so insecure that she doesn't begin the normal separation process from the parent. Such a child grows up lacking a sense of self or reality. She may even become deeply emotionally disturbed because she doesn't know who she is or what is expected of her.

Why all the emphasis on Mahler's *attachment process* in the first few years of life? Because once a nurturing mother or caretaker gives the two-year-old the vital emotional support she needs, along with the opportunity for autonomy, the child develops a sense of security and self-worth even when the mother is absent or angry. She has a clear sense of boundaries between herself and the mother and herself and the environment and a sure sense of trust that the loved one will return.

A *fear of abandonment* is one of the child's greatest concerns. When a child is abandoned, either emotionally or in actuality by desertion, she may grow up with a feeling that no relationship is secure. She always lives on the edge, clinging to a lover or a child, yet no assurance, no proof of stability, love, or good faith is ever enough. She may spend the rest of her life looking for someone to fill that desperate need.

In addition, babies who lack maternal nurturing or close human response in infancy may never build capacities for empathy, compassion, or intimacy. John Bowlby, in his studies of institutional deprivation in Great Britain, found that children raised in orphanages almost never learned to relate to others or to develop lasting attachments. These children also developed poor motor coordination and perceptual abilities. Many of them simply withered and die!

Fortunately for Ellen, she didn't wither or die. Far from it: she survived happily. Her salvation during those early years of childhood was in her vital, energetic, loving grandparents and great-grandparents!

Ellen: A Story with a Happy Ending

"What saved me, in spite of everything, was the adoration of my Norwegian grandparents—my father's parents," Ellen says, smiling as she recalls them.

"They were volatile, noisy, dramatic, and—unlike my mother's family—they loved women. I was born in their farmhouse and was the 'apple of my grandmother's eye.' Until my grandmother died when I was seven, we all lived together—not just my grandparents, parents, and me, but also my great-grandparents. Then, at Grandmother's death, everyone moved out. I didn't realize until later that I had lost everyone at once! Because we moved too, and I had to live with the 'evil witch,' my mother.

Then, at the same time, I started wearing glasses and I wasn't allowed to run around for fear of breaking them or of colliding with things. I suddenly became isolated and depressed. Actually, I was gloomy and depressed until I left therapy in my mid-forties—or that's my recollection. I guess it wasn't all gloom and doom though, because I've always had a sense of humor and I made great friends in art school."

TRIANGULATION: A DANGEROUS GAME

Let's look at the factors that intensified Ellen's unhappy situation.

First, *only males were valued in her maternal family* (just as they still are in many Oriental and Middle Eastern cultures). Her mother, growing up in a patriarchal family without a mother, felt that only men were dependable. This attitude was encouraged by the rigid British perception of women as helpless, frail human beings who die on you just at the time you need them the most!

Second, Ellen *was selected to bear the brunt of the family conflicts*—the hidden conflicts over money, lifestyle, and her mother's anger at the downturn her life had taken when Ellen was born. Since Ellen characterizes her mother as a probable near-psychotic, she probably would have been bitter and resentful no matter what opportunities opened up for her, but Ellen was a convenient *scapegoat* for her boundless misery, bearing the pressure of her parents' disappointment with each other and entering into a fierce conflict with her mother.

In Ellen's case we see Bowen's *classic triangular pattern*, with mother and daughter fused in an intense relationship and the father isolating himself from the family conflicts by remaining aloof and distant. This is what happens when two people marry who are emotionally dependent and are looking to each other to fulfill all their needs— needs that were never met in childhood. When a wife or husband fails to meet that impossible demand, we feel frustration and anger at the marital partner and reach out to another person for love, support, and companionship—or as an outlet for anger. Then a vulnerable person, usually a child, is pulled into the fray. Ellen's father may have found his isolated position at the far end of the triangle appealing since he was no longer the object of his volatile wife's wrath.

Ellen's family pattern illustrates the workings of the triangle:

Figure 2.2
Diagram of Ellen's Family Pattern

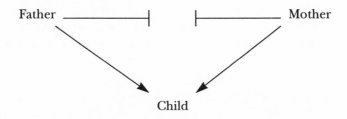

Source: M. Nichols, *Family Therapy: Concepts and Methods* (New York: Gardner Press, 1984).

With the focus on Ellen, her parents never had to voice their frustrations with each other or to take a critical look at the failure of their own lives. However, since her mother still felt her losses very keenly, Ellen became the outlet for a pent-up dam of explosive emotions.

If you met Ellen now, you would have no inkling that she was ever a depressed, fearful person. She is quick, light, and always on the move. You ask her a question and she is off and running, pausing only to laugh or to punctuate the conversation with an aside or question. But it has taken years of therapy and a network of friends and support groups for the real Ellen to emerge. It hasn't been easy for her to escape her mother's characterization of her as an unattractive, unlovable person who is a failure at anything she attempts.

How did Ellen overcome a traumatic childhood that might have led to a lonely, bitter life or even psychosis? In part we see the influence of the vital, adoring grandparents who passed on to her a basic optimism and resiliency. But other factors emerge as Ellen completes her story.

DEFEND YOUR BORDERS

"I thought that by removing myself physically from my parents' home, by marrying a man I loved, and beginning a family of my own, I could escape my maternal heritage, my parents, the hidebound aunts and uncles—all the old fossils from another era—but I really didn't. Without being aware of it, I was following the same old patterns that had made my childhood so unhappy. It wasn't until I went into a self-help group for parents called "Creative Problem Solving for Your Kids" that I began to realize there are other attitudes out there, other ways of dealing with issues rather than denying they were there at all or blaming someone else for whatever ails you.

I learned so much psychology from that parenting group (where incidentally I was ten to fifteen years older than a lot of the mothers because I had married so late) that I wanted to know more. I graduated from there to adult therapy groups.

From what I understand now, I think that my mother was *learning disabled.* She couldn't write a check, for instance. She would start at the bottom and work her way up to the top. I don't know if she finished eighth grade even. She didn't read or write well. And she couldn't follow directions or grasp abstract concepts.

But she had a lot of talents. She was an accomplished cook and everyone praised her for that and thought she was great. Yet she didn't have much of a self-image and couldn't take credit for the things she did do well, which was probably why she made my life so miserable. She claimed children didn't like her, and maybe they didn't because I don't think she liked them either—and me particularly."

REPEATING THE NEGATIVE PATTERN

"When my son was little," Ellen continues thoughtfully, her expressive face quiet, "we didn't make much of a fuss over him, just continued in our hidebound ways, the old Victorian values of 'a child should be seen and not heard.' He shouldn't even be seen too much! My husband is an unassuming man, a hard worker, who had been brought up with much the same Puritanical ideas that I had. We taught our son that you don't whine and complain. You do what you have to and if there's not a lot of joy in it, that's to be expected.

I remember we took him to the World's Fair in the sixties when he was just five and insisted that we go by bus—a long, arduous trip. We had a car, but we didn't think we should use it for frivolous purposes. We spent the whole day walking and exploring the fairgrounds, seeing everything we could. We expected him to keep up and never complain. Then we had to make the long trek back by bus. We were all exhausted and resentful.

Why did we have to make everything so hard for him and for ourselves? It never occurred to either my husband or myself that there was another way. With the car we could have turned the whole expedition into an adventure. We never even thought of making it fun!

When you start to change, though, there are a lot of reverberations. It was around this time that I had started with the parenting group, and then later with various therapy groups. Friends began saying to my husband, 'Isn't it wonderful how Ellen has changed?' But he didn't understand and neither did my son at first. They wanted me to stay the same. I would be in the kitchen doing dishes or cooking but in a place I no longer inhabited. It was strange.

Actually, your family doesn't want change. It makes everyone uncomfortable. I was the 'shy, quiet one.' I never caused trouble or stirred things up, and that way it was easy for everyone. But I couldn't stay in that state. Everything was bottled up inside me, ready to explode, my natural love of life and all the creative ideas I wanted to pursue—music, art, writing. Once the dam broke, there was no stopping it.

My mother's family, and consequently my mother, considered everything in life a catastrophe. But I think it's not what happens to you that matters but what you make of it. You don't have to be a victim or a scapegoat. The challenge is always there, and you can sink deeper and deeper into the old suffocating marsh of denial and repression, or you can respond by fighting back, by looking for new perceptions, new outlets for all that energy you put into being a victim."

YOU DON'T HAVE TO BE A VICTIM!

Although we can remove ourselves physically from our family systems, we may discover, as Bowen points out, that we bring unresolved problems with us. We bring feelings of suppression, resentment, and anger. We bring our dependency, helplessness, a whole framework of self-defeating feelings.

Even after her marriage, Ellen felt tightly bound to the joyless prescription of her maternal family, and began to bring up her son with the same harsh dictums that had made her own life so miserable. In order to solve her son's problems, she discovered—under the tutelage of a self-help parenting group—that there was a whole new realm of ideas and attitudes out there. Only then could she move out of the old *stuck* perceptions of her childhood upbringing.

Ellen discovered that *she had choices*. She could still look with sympathy at her mother and the forces that had shaped her—an early unhappy marriage, an unwanted pregnancy, her maternal grandparents' embittered thinking—and then move out of the emotional snare of her parents' relationship. But first she had to remove herself from that old repressive scene and step out of her role as victim.

RESOLVE OLD ISSUES

Sometimes when we suffer harsh, loveless childhoods like Ellen's we go through our adult lives with that emotional burden hung around our necks like an albatross. How often we imitate a parent who has made us miserable—simply because we don't know anything else. We have a parent who was an alcoholic, for example, so when we encounter problems, we have no way of knowing how to solve them constructively. At the same time we're feeling tremendous pain because living with an alcoholic is lonely, isolating, and shameful. We turn to alcohol as the only viable solution we know. Then we repeat the old pattern of despair and anger and pass it on to our children!

Ellen's parents were not alcoholics, but her mother was a near psychotic and her father distant and detached, and the forces released by the dysfunctional family system were equally as destructive.

Many of us have unresolved issues similar to Ellen's—issues of dependency, denial, or addiction and their attendant chaos and misery. If we fail to resolve our conflicts within the original family, our issues—like Ellen's—will continue to erupt in the marital relationship, and possibly even more intensely, in relationships with our children.

Ellen's mother died years ago, but it was still necessary for Ellen to come to terms with her unhappy legacy. With the help of a therapist and the support of many self-help groups, Ellen finds these steps have worked for her:

1. Forgive Mother (at least in part) by understanding her plight—an early unwanted pregnancy, the frustration of her dreams of a career.
2. Step away from the triangle—the unresolved tensions of her parents' relationship.
3. Put the focus back on her own life by expressing her feelings honestly.
4. Develop her creative life through painting, poetry, and drama.
5. Continue to seek the support of self-help and writing groups.
6. Defend her borders—stand up for her rights in every relationship.

AN OLD STORY WITH A NEW SCRIPT

Amy, a soft-spoken, attractive redhead in her early thirties, is, to all outward appearances, a success story. Poised, cultivated, and intelligent, she is a talented editor who works for a professional quarterly in Washington, D.C. Her possessions are few but choice—an antique dresser inherited from her mother's family, a golden retriever, and a houseful of books. Amy enjoys writing and dreams of going to graduate school to complete her Ph.D. in English literature. Amy, like Ellen, grew up in a household dominated by a dependent mother. But Amy's mother, Beth, was childlike and helpless rather than hostile and controlling like Ellen's.

ROLE REVERSAL TAKES ITS TOLL

"I was never a child," Amy says sadly. "At least, I don't think so. Mom was the baby in the family, and we all had to take care of her, my dad, my brother, and I. I was the one who felt most responsible, maybe because I was a girl. Or maybe I was just naturally sympathetic because Mom seemed so helpless.

You have to realize when you look at Mom, there's a lot of instability in her family, going back a long way. Her mother was an alcoholic and a prescription-drug addict who died when Mom was five years old. She took an overdose of drugs. We are still not sure if it was suicide or an accident. Mom's father was an alcoholic too, but he finally pulled himself out of that black hole after his wife's death. I think he finally stopped drinking—although it wasn't easy and didn't happen all at once. Later on, he married a stable, caring woman, E., who tried to give the household some direction.

But it was too late for Mom. Maybe she inherited those nervous tendencies or maybe they were a result of those early traumatic experiences. I don't know. I do know she never really grew up, still hasn't, except now she's worse than ever. Her health is going, and she's getting more and more paranoid every day. She lives alone and sometimes doesn't see a soul for days on end. There's a social worker who checks on her every week and a young neighborhood boy who comes by now and then, but that's about it.

She'll tell you herself that she's in bad shape, but she won't let me—or anyone—help her. She's an intelligent, witty person and was really beautiful when she was young. But she's a wreck now and still just in her fifties. She's scared to death of doctors and institutions and won't even go to the doctor when something is seriously wrong.

I think she did try to change. Just like her own mother, she had started drinking a lot—and maybe taking prescription drugs too—when my brother and I were little. We were born just a year apart, and Mom didn't know how to take care of herself—much less two small children who needed a lot of attention. Even though we had help, a woman who came in to take care of us during the day, she was overwhelmed.

My dad would take on a lot, but he was working full-time and couldn't be home to oversee everything. He bought the groceries, things like that. Mom was actually a wonderful cook. She'd cook these big meals, with fried chicken, corn on the cob, and collards, and then sit there, smoking a cigarette while the three of us ate. When my brother and I were really small, I picture Dad eating alone most of the time.

Finally things got to such a point that Mom had a breakdown and had to go away to a rehab center. She was there for several months, and to her credit, she stopped drinking then and started going to AA. It's funny. She liked being with people in AA, people who were as lost and confused as she was. I think she felt secure with them, and I believe basically, if she could have ever straightened out enough, she would have been good at working with them. But she never pulled herself together enough for that to succeed for long.

As my brother and I started to grow up, she became more and more dependent on us. This was very confusing for me, trying to sort out who I was. I didn't do well in grammar school, never made good grades or was outstanding in any way. I must have been in too much emotional turmoil, because in high school and college, I turned out to be something of a super student. It surprised me as much as anyone when I came out with a 650 score in the SATs for both English and math.

I didn't have many friends until later either, around junior high. I was moody and withdrawn as a kid, and everyone looked at me as the problem in the family. I didn't make friends that easily, and since I couldn't predict what kind of mood Mom would be in when I came home, I didn't bring anyone home often, if ever. When I did start to have friends finally in seventh or eighth grade, Mom was definitely starting to go 'round the bend.' My friends knew this, and we just didn't talk about it."

REVERSING GENERATIONAL ROLES

It's clear that Amy never enjoyed an opportunity to be a child. Her mother was searching desperately for someone to take care of *her!* Amy pulls out a photograph of a smiling mother holding out her arms to Amy, age six months.

"That was when *I* was still the baby and *she* the mother," Amy says, smiling ironically. "Here *I'm the mother.*" She points to a later photo of herself at age six, large blue eyes looking sadly at the camera, small sturdy hands holding the handlebars of her first bicycle.

Healthy families, according to Minuchin, are arranged hierarchically by generations. Each generation has a clearly defined role and position. Dysfunctional families like Amy's, Laura's, or Ellen's lack clear structure because a son or daughter is constantly forced to take the place of the missing parent and assume the role of an adult. Family therapists have a term for this unhappy role—*the parental child.* Such a child has no idea who she is or what is expected of her because she is burdened with the dual role of child and adult at the same time.

When the family hierarchy is disrupted by this fusion of the generations, we find destructive *cross-generational coalitions.* Amy sides with

Mom against Dad because Dad complains that Mom never cleans the house or has a meal ready on time. And Amy is busy trying to make up for all that Mom hasn't done and to protect her from Dad's anger. The more hidden these triangles, the more destructive they become, family therapist Jay Haley suggests, for they continue to work havoc in unseen configurations.

In families like Amy's, there is no time for the child to play with games or toys, or to spend time with friends—or even to make friends. There are always household tasks to be performed, dishes to wash, errands to run, often younger brothers or sisters to take care of. This top-heavy situation can cause the child a lot of anger and resentment, and when this parental child becomes an adult, she may repeat the pattern and demand that her child be a mother to her! The cycle perpetuates itself generation after generation in Bowen's multigenerational process until the chain is broken.

A child like Amy is stuck in an adult role without any of the accompanying privileges. Amy may be her mother's companion, advisor, and helper, but Mom still decides when Amy is to go to bed, which television programs she can watch, or if she can have a new dress. In such family systems the focus is always on Mom's problems. Mom can't sleep, can't eat, can't answer the phone, can't vacuum the living room. She is too tired or nervous or sick. Someone has to step into the spot vacated by Mom, and there's no time or energy left for Amy or her brother, William, to resolve their own problems. They can't even admit they have any.

When we treat a child as an adult, we not only violate *intergenerational boundaries*; we also invade *individual boundaries*. We take away the child's role by asking her to become an adult. When we confide in a daughter or son, we are expecting a child to communicate on an adult level, to give us the emotional sustenance we aren't getting from a husband or a lover. We see this happening especially at times of stress such as divorce or death. The child feels all-important for a while because she's so needed and Mom couldn't make it without her. But the bubble bursts when Mom finds a new boyfriend and she is dropped from the picture! She is left feeling isolated, lonely, and confused.

Experiential family therapists see troubled families as *emotionally dead.* The normal flow of behavior is blocked by unexpressed actions and feelings. Avoidance of feelings then leads to the development of symptoms in one or more family members, but these symptoms are often perceived as *normal* and therefore are invisible. When therapist

Carl Whitaker speaks of "the lonely father syndrome" or "the parental child," he is as concerned with these milder symptoms of dysfunction as with more extreme pathology.

THE CHILD: A BATTLEGROUND
FOR FEUDING PARENTS

According to current AA thinking, each member of the alcoholic family assumes a definite role—*the hero, the scapegoat, the clown,* and *the mascot.* The *hero* is the super achiever, outstanding in school and sports, popular with peers and teachers. The hero is designated to rescue the family name. In Amy's family her brother, William, took on the role of hero. An outstanding football player, an honor student throughout school, no one suspected, as Amy tells us, that "inside he was a little lost boy."

The *scapegoat* is the child with problems, who may be rebellious, truant from school, or even delinquent. Just as Ellen had become the scapegoat for her parents, Amy took on this role in her family, acting out the hidden conflicts between the parents and drawing the spotlight away from the real issues of resentment and antagonism between them. As a child, Amy was sullen and withdrawn, had few friends, and made poor grades in school. No one thought to look at Mom and her childish tantrums, her refusal to accept adult responsibilities.

The *clown,* as the name suggests, draws attention from the family issues by laughing, mocking, and making light of everything—while the *mascot* is the quiet unassuming child who retreats into a lonely, isolated existence. A son or daughter often plays one or more roles in the interactions of the system and can combine characteristics of one role with another. In addition to her role as scapegoat, Amy was also the mascot, withdrawing in loneliness and confusion whenever she felt overwhelmed. As she grew into maturity, she would also become the hero, excelling in her studies, taking on the family responsibilities, and trying to guard Mom's frail mental and physical health.

Because of the striking similarities—the failure to assume responsibility, and the denial, repression, and mixed messages inherent in the makeup of every dysfunctional family—these roles appear to be equally applicable to every unhealthy family system and are just as fitting in analyzing Ellen's or Amy's role as they are in assessing Laura's, where the alcoholic was the central pathological figure.

LIFE AMONG THE SAMOANS

"Mom's judgment wasn't good enough for me to rely on," Amy says quietly, "and Dad was uninvolved, so I didn't tell them about important things. Dad wasn't there, physically speaking, a lot of the time. He was busy trying to get his new business going, and I'm sure he must have been terribly worried about that at the time.

I didn't go to either one of them with problems unless I absolutely had to. Dad thought we should figure things out for ourselves, my brother and I; sometimes I just wanted him to act like a father and tell us what we should do. Mom was hopeless. We both knew that.

We didn't track each other's emotions either. No one ever asked me if I was happy or sad or worried. If I didn't do well in school, Mom would stick up for me when I was in the wrong. It really bothered me that she did because I knew I couldn't count on her judgment.

But Mom was always generous—in fact, had no concept of money at all—and she would give us $20 to go out to the mall or a restaurant. That was a lot of money to me in those days.

It was okay to make mistakes most of the time because my parents weren't that close to what was happening, usually didn't even know what was going on. In conversation, though, I had to say the 'right' thing, give the intelligent answer. This was mostly Dad, I think.

I didn't dare express what I felt to Mom because, again, I couldn't trust her judgment. She was too emotional and would get all worked up over something trivial or hold a grudge when I had forgotten the whole incident that caused the trouble. She came up with some wild solutions too. Plus the fact that I didn't tell her or Dad anything because I wanted them to approve of me and think I was perfect. My brother was always so terrific, great grades, popular with his friends, good in sports. Inside he was lost, but that didn't show.

On the other hand, even though no one seemed to notice if my shoes were worn out, Mom was not a respecter of privacy or possessions. On a whim she would appropriate something of mine—the most flagrant example is when she gave my TV set away to the maid! There were other instances too. I think she read my letters and diary all the time. One experience I remember vividly, which was such a silly thing and seems really funny now, but it didn't then. I asked her to mail a letter to some rock star. I had read he was having marital problems, and I sent him an article on 'intimate relationships.' Can you believe it? Anyway, Mom never got around to mailing it because it was still sitting on my dresser later that week. I could see she had unsealed the envelope and glued it back together.

After my parents got the divorce, when I was around fourteen, I lived with Mom; she was bitter and unhappy, a little crazy too. She complained all the time about money and her ex-husband, who happened to be my father. She felt vengeful even though she hadn't done much to keep the relationship going. She didn't see *that*, of course. I remember she set a pair of pink flamingos on the lawn in front of our townhouse just to embarrass Dad, who always prided himself on having impeccable taste. She didn't have any perspective or capacity for realizing her part in the whole mess. And since she was furious at Dad, she wanted us to hate him too. She certainly succeeded in turning me against him for a while. They sent me away to boarding school for a year at that point, which may have helped me retain my sanity.

I always felt uncertain about lots of things—clothes, for example. I would have to count on my grandmother, Dad's mother, who was a great support for me all along, to buy me clothes. Mom never noticed when I outgrew my clothes or when the seasons changed, and of course Dad didn't. He was too busy. After the divorce it was really tough. I never had a winter coat because I thought that was an extravagance. It's a lucky thing we lived in a warm climate! My grandmother would take me shopping once or twice a year, a lifesaver. I've never liked to ask for anything."

Strangely, though no one was aware of Amy's emotional wants or practical needs, she had little privacy. Her mother slipped into her bedroom, looked through her books and journal, and even read her sealed letters. On a whim, she even gave Amy's TV set away—without ever asking her.

Amy wished that her father could move in closer—tell her what to do, see that she had new clothes when she outgrew the old ones, help her with school projects, talk to her about what was happening in the family. But although Amy knew he cared about her, he set up his defenses against the turmoil by retreating. He established rigid individual boundaries that protected him from being hurt, and he couldn't let anyone, even his children, get too close!

Amy desperately needed someone to talk to about her feelings and everyday experiences, someone who could give her guidance and direction as well as affection. She did have her grandparents, but she didn't want to upset them by telling them just how bad things were. She didn't even want to ask for a winter coat!

ALWAYS A CARETAKER?

So engrained is Amy's role of looking after Mom that up until her mother's recent death she was racked with anxiety, spending sleepless nights worrying about Mom's loneliness, her poor health. Now she has extended her role of caretaker to the whole of humanity. She worries about everyone—friends, relatives, business associates, the children of Somalia.

"If I go to a meeting or a luncheon, I feel responsible for every person in the room with me," Amy relates. "I'm anxious if I think others are left out or neglected. I know this is ridiculous and illogical, but I can't seem to help myself. Maybe it's because I always had to take care of Mom. From the time I was a little girl I understood this. I knew she needed looking after, and I loved her and wanted to do everything I could to help her."

A mother like Amy's can be fragile and appealing—though cruel and demanding as well—and the child naturally wants to protect her. After all, the mother is the center of her life, and what would she do if this needy angel suddenly disappeared?

At a point in her adult life, when she would have liked to shake free of the demons that haunted her childhood, Amy found she couldn't relinquish the feeling that she, and she alone, was responsible for her mother's welfare. She would look at her mother's deteriorating mental and physical health and feel anguish and frustration, but there was little she could do—short of getting a court order and having this helpless (but resistant) woman carted off to a state institution. Like many of us in similar situations, Amy was slow to learn that no matter how much we love and pity a mother or son or daughter, we can't control their lives. And we only make ourselves miserable trying. A difficult lesson!

SHORING UP OUR BOUNDARIES

How has Amy been transformed into the strong, compassionate young woman we see now? First, she received early nurturing from a wonderful nurse who cared for her and her brother daily when they were toddlers. She made long visits in the summer and during vacations with her paternal grandparents, who were not only caring individuals but who talked about ideas and issues and loved literature, the arts, and music.

"When I was just a little girl," Amy relates, "my grandmother would spend hours reading to me. Peter Pan, Winnie the Pooh, the Bertram books. I grew up loving the old favorites. I still do."

As she moved into adolescence, she gradually began to realize that she was not only gifted with a quick intelligence, but was attractive as well, with a blossoming figure and a lovely face, high cheekbones, and hazel eyes. All those years of being responsible for Mom had taught her competence and organization too.

Now under the guidance of a professional therapist, these are the steps Amy is taking to shake herself free of her childhood role:

1. She allows others to take responsibility for their own actions.
2. She recognizes that caring does not mean caretaking—that although we care deeply, we can't control another person's choices or behavior.
3. She steps away from the family tensions by using her time and energy to resolve her own problems.
4. She sets limits in her relationships by standing up for herself and learning to say "no."

A HERITAGE OF CONFUSION AND RESENTMENT

As they grow up, what happens to these children who are Mother's (or Father's) *little sister, little man, little woman, little mother?* Ellen, who has come a long way from the dependency and helplessness fostered by her upbringing, is careful to stay far away from the emotional intensity of the parental network. Her parents are both dead now, but her feelings about them and the perceptions engendered during a loveless childhood don't disappear easily. She has to guard herself closely to be sure she doesn't slip back into feelings of self-doubt and blame.

Amy has to constantly struggle against feelings of over-responsibility—the feeling that she can somehow control the fate of humanity! She is beginning to realize that the more she focuses on others' problems, the less she succeeds at solving her own. On beginning a serious relationship with a man she respects and loves, she became more and more aware that she couln't afford to become so entangled in her mother's pain that she had no energy left for living her own life. She could be caring and supportive and still allow her mother to make decisions for herself—no matter how inadequate those choices may have been.

On the other hand, the *parental child* may refuse to grow up and demand that her husband or child take care of her, perpetuating the cycle of dependency. She may turn to drugs or alcohol as a way of alleviating her pain and grief. Or like Laura, Ellen, and Amy, she may begin to come to terms with her loss and anger, functioning as an independent yet caring person, all the while mourning her lost childhood.

> Red-winged blackbirds
> insistent after a long winter
> call love or pride or yearning.
> They wonder where
> I will wander
> when the path ends
> without warning
> when dust from my shoes
> still sings *go on, go on.*
>
> —"Cold Island"

3

Mermaid's Song

In your family you spoke in whispers,
sometimes long after midnight
wrote messages in code,
"I'm lonely, I'm afraid,"
and when your brother
seasons later
dropped the comic mask,
shouted, claimed he was angry,
you felt strange
as if your bones were open, lined with salt.

After that, you preferred to stay underwater,
far below the surface
of the algae-laden pond
across the road.
If it was dark there, a little lonely,
if the frogs croaked
too hoarsely or too long,
you liked the solitary moments,
rose stones that lined your bed.

And when you came up for air
(as you did from time to time)
if people stared
at your blemished tail
something like a mermaid's,
something like a spotted bream's,
they loved your purple fins,
your gills of gold.

—"Mermaid's Song"

"My Mother was a child-woman, mostly child," Shelley says, her expressive face reflective. "Mother stopped growing emotionally, never really matured, but stayed a ten-year-old. She was uneducated and never learned to read or write—in any language as far as I know. She had lived through chaos and tragedy, growing up in the Ukraine around the time of the Russian Revolution, had seen her two teenage brothers killed during that conflict and ensuing chaos. Maybe because she had seen so much horror she couldn't face the reality of becoming a woman.

I always felt that I had to take care of her. My father was rarely home, and when he was, he was not protective but was a strong man with a violent temper. I remember very clearly being afraid of him. Mother was afraid of him and everything else.

Her own parents had fled, escaping the purges at home, when she was an adolescent. They lived in Paris for a year or so and then came here to this country with my mother, the oldest living child, and a younger brother and sister.

I was aware from the time I can remember that our family was different from other families. There was no center, no closeness. As an adult, I discovered why, I think. There was somebody else my father loved, and he wanted to leave us but couldn't. We (my two brothers and I) managed to keep him in a marriage he hated. I found out much later that when I was about two years old, my father left and then found that my mother was pregnant with my younger brother. So he had no choice but to come back to us.

Also my father came from an angry, bitter family. They wanted him to get an education and when he wasn't interested, there were terrible arguments. He had left home at fifteen to escape that scene."

THE FAMILY HERITAGE: DISTANCE AND RIGIDITY

Shelley is an animated, highly articulate woman who has combined multiple careers as a teacher, lawyer, and writer. In every area she has been highly successful, and now that she is semi-retired from her business career, she continues to give lectures, work with a number of philanthropic organizations, and write novels and poetry. But—yes, there is always a "but" in the lives of the remarkable women represented in these pages—Shelley has survived a childhood of harsh neglect and deprivation to become the person she is today.

Shelley's family gives us a casebook example of *rigid individual and family boundaries.* Shelley, her two brothers, and mother and father appeared to exist in separate spheres with almost no interaction between them. There was no affection or closeness between the mother and father—the father a product of an angry, dissident background and the mother's emotional growth stunted by tragedy when she was still a young girl. Even with her children, Shelley tells us, her mother failed to demonstrate any affection, any sharing of ideas and feelings. Unlike most rigid families, however, where the central motivating factor that holds them together is achievement and ambition, Shelley's parents offered little in the way of encouragement or guidance.

"No, I never felt free to express my feelings or ideas," Shelley continues. "In fact, it wouldn't have occurred to me that I could. No one would have listened. I was a reader practically from birth, I believe. I taught myself to read when I was three years old, and from then on I lived in my own world with a rich fantasy life.

My parents definitely didn't confide in me. With their background and that generation, I don't believe they could have. I have a memory of when I was around five. My mother was sitting in a chair crying because my father was very late coming home. I said to her 'I hate him!' And she replied, 'You can't hate him. He is your father.' That is the only thing I remember her saying to me. I don't remember ever being held or kissed by either parent.

I had little existence as far as my parents were concerned. Even if they had seen my diaries or personal letters as I was growing up, I don't think they would have been interested. There was no connection, no awareness of an emotional bond. And I never knew my father's parents or relatives. They were all killed in the Holocaust.

I don't remember ever speaking to my father, having a real conversation with him. He simply wasn't interested and couldn't be bothered. With my mother it had always been out of the question. I have no idea what my parents' opinions were, and certainly my ideas didn't interest them. People who knew my father well describe him as a man of warmth and friendliness. I never saw that. We children were anchors who held him down. I think you have to look at it from an adult point of view and I do. I don't feel bitterness. I think there are very few real monsters out there.

If I felt sick as a child, I called the doctor myself. And then I went in to see him if I needed to. On the other hand, when I got my period at thirteen or fourteen, I had no idea what was happening. I thought it must be a terrible accident or sickness.

I did *everything* for myself. There was no one else. Even when Mother was alive I felt I had my real life with a curtain up between us. I always felt estranged. At my home there was no one to talk to. It was just a place to eat and sleep. Later on there was very little food even—it was only a place to sleep."

THE RESILIENT CHILD—A SURVIVOR

What kind of nurturance or affection could Shelley have ever received with such an upbringing? Very little, it seems. Her father not only was cold and distant, but was an angry violent man who showed little or no interest in his children. Shelley has a few recollections of Mother, but she can't remember her mother holding her even as an infant— comforting her, laughing with her, telling her stories. She knew from the beginning that it was up to her to be totally self-reliant. There was no one else!

Shelley appears to defy all we know of Mahler's attachment theory— a theory that is validated by the studies of Mary Ainsworth, Bowlby, and others, demonstrating the importance of nurturance and affection in our early lives. By all rights, according to psychological theory, Shelley should have become a helplessly dependent person like her mother with little sense of identity. Or with the kind of physical and emotional neglect she experienced, she might have become a psychotic or a drug addict or a criminal. How can we account for her super achievements?

Psychologist Emmy Werner in a longitudinal study of children of Kauai discovered that some children are naturally resilient—these children, even when born into poverty, possess inborn traits that give them strength and protection. Such babies are perceived of as good-natured or *easy babies*. They are often firstborn children, have a relatively high tolerance for pain and frustration, and have the ability to recover quickly from conflict and difficulty.

We can surmise that Shelley was by any standards a remarkably resilient child. Bright, imaginative, and resourceful, she knew to call the doctor if she were sick, to forage for food if she were hungry, to read and study when she was left alone, and to use her considerable intellectual gifts to become an outstanding student. Soon she would need all her survival skills for a loss that would destroy any semblance of happiness or security in her life.

ALL IS BLEAK AND DARK

"I can't remember exactly when my mother died," Shelley says softly, "but I know I was still in elementary school. While my mother was still alive there are some 'sun dappled memories.' We had friends and family over to our apartment at times; there was food in the house. But after that it was all bleak and dark.

My mother's parents were lovely people, but they lived across the city, which in those days was a continent away as they had no car and almost no money. My grandfather died when I was four, and there was a sharp division in my life from my mother's illness on. I used to wonder later (when I was in my thirties) about my grandmother, why she didn't take me in after my mother's death. I just found out recently that she had wanted to come live with us then and my father refused. I heard that she used to cry and cry. It must have been a terrible grief for her—to lose my mother and then all contact with me or my brothers. Maybe my father didn't want her to visit us either. I don't know.

After Mother died, I never saw my father or my two brothers. I think my older brother (who was five years older than I) may have been away at school. Even now I don't really know. That's how distant we were. My younger brother stayed with one of his friends from school; a family living in the low-cost housing projects took him in. They had no money, but they were rich—rich in love and caring. That friend has turned out to be extraordinarily successful, by the way.

But I wasn't aware of what was happening at the time. I was encapsulated in my own world, living a separate life. I couldn't stand looking at reality. The place where we lived was so awful. It was an apartment in the inner city, and it was dirty and bleak. The plaster was falling, and it was infested with vermin. There was never enough food either, especially on the weekends.

There was a woman who came in to clean for us, but she never did any cleaning. My father would leave money for her to buy groceries, but I suspect that she pocketed most of it. On weekends I often had to steal because there was nothing left and my father was always gone. I would steal soda bottles to make money for food. I went to a variety of supermarkets so no one would notice and I stayed close to strange women, hoping that the clerks would think I belonged to them.

As I was growing up, I had no responsibilities, no chores. There was no one to supervise me or to look after me either except for that indifferent woman who came in at times. My father never checked to see if I had money, food, or clothes, anything. Later on, in my teens, I would ask for money, and I bought clothes and food for myself—my choices were not always the best either as you can imagine. I would write a note asking for money and sometimes my father would leave it, sometimes not. I never saw him. Where was he? Staying with the woman he later married, I imagine, although I'm not really certain.

Escape into my fantasy world was my salvation. What would I have done without books? I don't think I would have made it. I have to tell you that I thought then that I was lucky because I had no rules. No one cared what I did. I made every decision for myself, and I did precisely what I wanted—as far as I was able to.

I was always a good student. I remember being very anxious the first day of a new grade. I wanted to be sure the teacher recognized that I was the smartest in the class. This is how I measured my own worth."

SHELLEY'S STORY: DEPRIVATION, NEGLECT, AND TRIUMPH!

Shelley has trouble remembering exactly when her mother died or what happened to her brothers after her mother's death; probably she has repressed whole periods of her childhood that are too painful to recall. But, in fact, Shelley throughout her life, appears to have had the capacity for a considerable degree of detachment from the abandonment that could have left her emotionally damaged. She does remember the dirty, disheveled apartment where she lived and that her father was never home, even on weekends, and that he didn't provide enough food to last the weekend. In fact, it seems his petite, intelligent daughter didn't even exist for him.

Yet Shelley, from the time she was three, had another world at her command—the world of fantasy and imagination, the world of books. Her remarkable intellect and curiosity enabled her to separate the harsh, real world from a soaring, imaginative world where anything is possible. It's almost as if the events that she experienced in her dark, isolated childhood were part of a fascinating book she was reading.

Somehow, though, she never slipped totally into unreality—or made the descent into schizophrenia and madness. Shelley believes that several wonderful women may have saved her from such a fate—*mentors* who brought hope and light into her bleak universe.

"If ever I were to believe in God it would be because at every critical point in my life, there has been a mentor. The first was my kindergarten teacher. She kept me back in kindergarten for another year because my motor skills were so poor. I could read almost anything, but I couldn't hold a pencil properly. But she told me she kept me for two years because she loved me so much.

My second-grade teacher was amazing. She had memorized Dickens—*David Copperfield, Great Expectations, Oliver Twist*—and every afternoon she would read to us. Yet she was really not reading, but quoting whole passages from memory. She gave me my first love of great literature.

I had a right to my own possessions, I believe, but I had so few that they didn't mean anything. I had five or six books that I really cherished. My chief possession was my library card, and that was all I really cared about."

INVASIONS FOR SHELLEY—A NEW CATEGORY

How, you may ask, did Shelley suffer boundary invasions? Her parents were so indifferent to her very existence that they never asked about feelings, her ambitions, her ideas for the future. They didn't care enough to invade her privacy or look into her letters and journals. Later after her mother died, her father never even knew if she were hungry or sick. Emotional and physical neglect is as much a form of abuse as is overt abuse. Both are forms of boundary invasions—turning the child's world upside down, forcing her to take on an adult role and to defend herself against poverty and indifference.

Dr. Vincent Fontana, in his groundbreaking account of child abuse, *Somewhere a Child Is Crying,* first published in 1973, recognized a pattern that he calls "active neglect." Children in this category have been starved of all affection, encouragement, and care. In treating these neglected children at the New York Foundling Hospital, Fontana found they were dull, unresponsive, and lethargic. Many were emaciated or dehydrated, and had been given inappropriate medication (or no medication at all); infections went untreated. These "children of neglect" never laughed and seldom even cried. Fontana and his colleagues found there was little actual difference between abuse and neglect when it came to the tragic consequences of such mistreatment. Shelley, except for her exceptional inner resources, might have been one of these pathetic waifs.

Can we consider active neglect to be a boundary invasion? We definitely can because neglect has many manifestations. One study of abused and neglected children found that these youngsters are likely to lack trust in relationships and to attribute hostile attitudes to others since they grow up feeling that the world is an unpredictable place where every individual must fight desperately to survive. Such children may also suffer failures in interpersonal relationships as they develop feelings of abandonment and loneliness—often precursors of clinical depression in adulthood. The shadow of such deep-seated feelings, Shelley's "well of sadness," continues to haunt her even today despite her brilliant career and fulfilling marriage.

With Shelley we witness another familiar boundary invasion—the reversal of generational roles. Like Amy, Shelley, almost from birth, was aware that her mother was a fragile, childish woman who needed protection from the harsh realities of poverty and loss. And the mother also needed protection from her husband, Shelley's father, who frightened and oppressed her! Shelley doesn't remember if her two brothers sided with her mother, but we can imagine that they did when we examine the hostile, neglectful father figure Shelley depicts.

If we were to draw a diagram of the family triangulation, we would show Shelley and her two brothers at a point close to the mother and far distant from the father. But the lines between all members of the family would be rigid or disengaged, with little support, communication, or bonding between any of the members. After the mother's death the boundary lines for the three siblings grow far apart both physically and emotionally. Shelley even has difficulty remembering where her brothers were living at this stage of her life.

Shelley's family also displays rigid *external boundary lines,* which means that the family had little contact or communication with the outside world. There was almost no intermingling with friends, no activities that bound them to the school or community; even Shelley's maternal grandparents were seldom allowed into the family inner circle. So Shelley lived a life of increasing isolation and loneliness. This is how she describes the family scene:

"It wasn't possible to have friends. I couldn't bring anyone home. Our home was a dungeon. I couldn't dream of making a friendship reciprocal so I didn't try. I was very introverted. I suspect I was even a *scowling introvert*. Under my high school yearbook the caption reads one word—*disappearing*. I wanted to be invisible and I almost was—an alienated person. I didn't allow anyone behind the mask until I met G., my husband, and he has been my mentor above all others and from that time on. But I'm getting ahead of my story.

Oddly enough, I found that life of my childhood exciting and free, a challenge. I even felt sorry for other children who had to be home by a certain time, who had to live by rules. On the other hand, if I saw a mother and daughter together, I would try to stand near them to discover what their relationship was. I had no idea of a real relationship. I remember climbing up, looking into other people's windows to find out what families were like. To me that was like reading another book. I don't remember feeling sad. I only remember intense curiosity.

I don't recall either of my parents asking to see a report card. Possibly they signed my reports, which were always all 'A's' until my freshman year in high school. But there was no interest in who I wanted to be, what my hopes and ambitions were, and if I wanted to go to college. I realized very early that I was on my own.

I have few happy memories although I think I am naturally a happy person. A happy person operating out of a deep well of sadness."

Was Shelley the bearer of the family's loss? We can't be certain as this was a family so detached from feeling as to be almost psychotic, or at least pathologically void, but we do know that Shelley was the child selected to stay on with the father after her mother's death. And certainly she would bear the brunt of his pain, anger, and neglect.

Her lack of bitterness and generous attitude of forgiveness and compassion toward her father constitute an amazing leap toward acceptance and growth. Sustained by years of therapy and a growing sense of self-fulfillment, she is able to look at her father and recognize the forces that shaped and distorted him. She realizes that "there are few real monsters" among us.

As Shelley grew into adolescence and young womanhood, she would find formidable challenges but unexpected gifts as well.

A SYMBOL OF HOPE: LIGHT IN THE SHADOWS

"I was elected vice-president of my class in eighth grade. I can't imagine why because I had no friends—none. And I was the ultra 'uncool kid,' the way I dressed or talked. It must have been some kind of tribute to my intelligence.

But I dropped out of school in the middle of my freshman year in high school. I had always gotten straight 'A's' throughout school, and that year I was on the super honor roll. We lived in a fairly prosperous section of L., but our apartment was a shambles. It had never been furnished. And I had no clothes either, at least practically none.

That freshman year two events came together—the Honor Society planned to make a trip into the city and I had nothing suitable to wear. I simply couldn't go and that was a great disappointment to me. About a month later I wrote an anti-establishment essay, and the principal told me I had a 'warped mind.' That kind of rejection really stunned me. The last half of that year I stopped studying or going to class or doing my homework, and I made straight 'F's.' This was in the public schools. But my IQ was so high that there were authorities who didn't want to let me go. They arranged for me to attend a unique private school for girls that was perfect for me, very nurturing. I learned grace and manners there. We stood up when an adult came in the room and remained standing in the cafeteria until everyone was seated. We curtsied to the headmaster.

There were only six students in my class. The headmaster was a soft-spoken man, very gentle, very scholarly. We were encouraged to read everything, and it covered an incredible range—Carlyle, Ruskin, Chaucer, Shakespeare. I remember memorizing a large chunk of Burke's "Conciliation with America." This is where I built my foundation for all the study I would do later in college and graduate school.

The school had been built in the mid-1900s and was a wonderful old stone mansion with huge fireplaces in many of the rooms and a great staircase leading up to the third floor where art classes were held and down two stories to a spacious basement for ceramics workshops.

The school hadn't changed that much from the time it was built and was very British. We observed "elevenses"—that is tea and biscuits at 11:00 A.M. And we studied two years of British history with only one year of American. This was a gentle environment that gave me intellectual and emotional sustenance. These years of high school in a sense saved my life. This has been true most of my life—when things were really desperate, something or somebody turned up, a savior of some kind.

It didn't matter there that I was from such a different background. The other girls were all from affluent families, but we wore uniforms and no makeup so we all looked alike. And I waited on a main street for the cab that picked us up from different sections of the city and suburbs.

I had a partial scholarship, and my father raised the money for me to go to the school. He had no choice since during my freshman year, after the crisis with the principal, I had stopped going to school. It wasn't because he cared about what happened to me or knew me as a person at all. Pirandello says 'life is full of infinite absurdities which have to be plausible because they are true.'

The headmaster had a degree in classics from Princeton University. He was a strong, gentle presence, particularly for someone like me who had only seen working-class men who weren't polished or educated. He was the Latin Master and the class met in a large library with glass bookcases and a Persian carpet. In the winter there was usually a fire going in the enormous stone fireplace. It was almost a mythic kind of atmosphere.

The teachers and staff were interested in you, and you could have one-on-one relationships with them. For the first time since elementary school I saw women I admired—educated, smart, caring. I had a teacher there who was an extraordinary woman, a person of innate elegance. She was different from anyone I'd ever known, aristocratic, Episcopalian, and descended from someone who came over on the *Mayflower,* I think. I'm Jewish and my mother and her parents were fleeing persecution from the powers that be. Maybe it's not that different after all since the Pilgrims were fleeing persecution too.

From this teacher I saw that it was possible to 'be somebody.' She was probably my most important mentor of all. From this time on I recognized that my intellectual gifts were a source not only of survival but of doors opening and letting the light in.

Light has always been a symbol of hope and transcendence to me. There was a place not too far from where I lived in the inner city. It was a little village almost right in the middle of the city, with small bungalows set in a communal lawn. There was one front yard and little paths leading to the houses. On the way to school one day I saw a shaft of sunlight that was liquid gold. Two children were caught in that light and their bodies were burnished. I remember thinking that if only I could get into that sunlight, I could enter a totally changed world. Yet there was something that frightened me about that vision—

maybe the intensity of it or a sadness beneath the beauty of it. I went back again and again searching for that experience, but I never found it.

My take on life is very different from that of everyone I know. I see things from the point of view of a deprived person. I am sensitive to things that others may not be aware of—how people speak to someone they consider to be an inferior class, for example. I have an incredible aversion to any kind of bigotry—financial, racial, religious, but certainly in terms of class. I am aware of the shades and nuances of conversation. The subtext—what isn't spoken—I feel is far more important. Reality is in the subtext.

Sometimes I wonder what I would have done if I had had a happy childhood. Maybe I would be an obese housewife eating chocolates. I was driven to achieve—*to impress on myself that I was a worthwhile person.*"

SHELLEY'S STORY—IT DEFIES THE THEORISTS

Psychoanalyst Erik Erikson suggests that the ego develops through an internal process that includes a consolidation of inner structures and images. He proposes that these identifications, along with our social roles, form the basis for ego identity. Protected by a basic trust in the mother or caretaker, the growing child can face unfamiliar situations with confidence; without that sense of trust new situations evoke fear and apprehension. But psychologist E. Jacobson points out that our internal images never correspond exactly to reality but reflect our subjective experiences. In Shelley's case we can only surmise that her inner world of fantasy and imagination, along with her own innate strength, enabled her to form positive images of a world of optimism and light.

Then at a crucial turning point when even the trusted life of school seemed to be turning against her, she would discover a whole new universe opening up—inside the halls of a superior private school. There she would find an atmosphere of curiosity, a respect for learning, a broad spectrum of knowledge, and a new mentor, a teacher who would reveal to her all the options open to her through the quests of the intellect.

Shelley perceives her view of life to be shaped by her childhood background of deprivation, but, according to psychological theory, the exact opposite is often the case. Children like Shelley who fail to develop a secure sense of attachment are usually lacking in empathy, the quality that enables us to put ourselves in another person's place and experience related emotions. To account for her deeply humanitarian views and her continuing work with the underprivileged, I believe we have to look at Shelley's intellectual gifts, the influences of her nurturing private school, and the wide range of studies that have opened up many different worlds for her. Shelley is also an artist, with the sensitivity and imagination that nourish her creativity.

ESCAPE INTO EARLY MARRIAGE: LIVING A LIFE OUTSIDE

"When I was a senior in high school, my father announced that he was going to be married again and that there was literally no room in his life or his home for two women—not that there had ever been much room for me. So I was pushed into marriage with my first husband, but it was never a real marriage. I lived my life outside that relationship.

During the years of my marriage I compartmentalized my life in the world and my life at home. My real life was going to graduate school where I got my Ph.D. in political science. Then I decided I needed more than that to make a difference in the world, and I went back to school and got a law degree—ten years after the Ph.D. I had very intense friendships in graduate school and in law school, but even there I divided my lives—my friends from graduate school didn't know my friends from law school. And none of them knew my husband or anything about my life with him.

Wherever I was, I saw myself as an observer, almost a subversive. I was very different from my first husband. He would say he knew exactly 'what I was thinking,' and I would be incapable of that kind of thinking! This marriage was an escape—I thought, a necessity. It never occurred to me to get an apartment of my own and live on my own (which I had always done to a large extent anyway). But women I knew at that point in my community didn't live independently. They stayed at home until they were married. I didn't know anything else was an option just as for years after I was married, I never considered a divorce. That wasn't a choice that entered my mind.

During this marriage of twenty-odd years I always worked full-time. And once I started writing college textbooks, I was earning quite a bit of money and turning it all over to my husband. No, I didn't do it because he demanded it but because then I felt free. I didn't have to deal with money or financial matters. It was a kind of unwritten contract with him. He had the money, and I essentially could do what I wanted, traveling into the city, having meetings with editors, working on manuscripts.

When I finally did decide to leave my husband, I took full responsibility for myself and for our two children's education. That meant four years of college for one son plus college and six years of graduate school for my other son. But I never doubted my ability to give them that. I had always worked seven days and nights, going to school, teaching, and writing, and I knew I could continue to. My husband and I had no outside life. We never went out to dinner or out with friends or on vacation. It was a confining life, but I didn't want to be with him so I didn't mind. Basically, all I did was work—and I always made sure I took care of my children.

My sons were the first people I remember loving, and I think I was overprotective of them. It was hard for me to set rules although I did. I would think, 'Is this what a real mother would do?' Because I had never seen how real families behaved, I had to make it up as I went along. But I always adored my children, and fortunately, they were great kids."

Just as Shelley had always divided her real life from the life she lived in books and fantasy, she would continue to juggle two distinct lives—or even three or four—as a wife and mother on the one hand and as a teacher, lawyer, and author on the other. Her real life would be with her studies and career; with her husband she would maintain the same rigid boundaries that she had known as a child that allowed for little intimacy or involvement. But with her children, whom she loved deeply, the boundaries were flexible, permitting warmth, love, and communication without encouraging overdependency and helplessness. Shelley knew very well the importance of self-reliance, but despite her own loveless childhood, she instinctively felt a deep bond of affection with her sons and was able to give them the nurturing so lacking in her own upbringing.

According to psychologist Julius Rotter, people who feel their fate is controlled by chance or outside forces have an *external locus of control*. Individuals like Shelley, who feel that they control their own destiny, perceive an *internal locus of control*. Such individuals have what social learning theorist Albert Bandura calls a *sense of self-efficacy* and are more persistent, less anxious, and more academically successful.

Shelley's sense of identity was based almost entirely on her own achievements for these were requisite for her to prove to herself that she was a "worthwhile person."

Shelley's character, even as a small child, appears to reflect a heightened capacity for risk taking. Although at times she must have been fearful and hesitant, she seemed in general to see her life as a colorful adventure. She felt she was lucky that she had no rules, no one to answer to. She loved the freedom of making decisions for herself and, instead of feeling self-pity that she was alone and neglected, she enjoyed peering into other people's lives, literally climbing up and looking into their windows to see how they talked and interacted with each other. She even appeared to feel that going out on the week-ends and stealing food was part of a dramatic narrative in which she starred. But she was clever enough to know that shop owners would not share her perspective, so she developed a strategy for staying close to strange families to avoid suspicion.

When I remarked to Shelley how resourceful she was, she only laughs and says, "I was a wild one but I didn't care. In fact, I even thought it was fun."

A LEGACY OF CHILDHOOD: DEPRESSION

Shelley's life would continue to be filled with challenges as she finally realized that her marriage was totally empty and that if she ever were to find any kind of fulfillment, she would have to take a long leap forward.

"When I finally decided to leave and divorce my first husband, I didn't expect to ever marry again. Then I met G., and my life turned around. He has been my great mentor ever since that time. I didn't think until then that there was such a thing as a happy family.

Today I have children who are accomplished and loving. I have wonderful grandchildren. And I have a husband I adore and who adores me. He is an unusual man with great understanding. I don't think I would have survived without him. But there is nothing anyone can do to hold back the depressions that strike me suddenly and with such force—even though I think that everything I had to be anxious about has already occurred!

I have always walked around feeling there was a great empty space inside. There is a sculptor who carves figures of people with vacant spaces and that reflects my experience. I am subject to depressions so deep and dark that my husband is shocked. They don't last long and probably come to a total of only about ten days a year.

Nothing grows there in that tunnel of despair. The pain is so intense I can barely describe it. Susan Lowenstein has created sculptures of the Lockerbie airline crash, huge sculptures of women in the postures of anguish they felt on learning that a son or daughter had died. That explosion over Scotland was so overwhelming and so terrible, with all those young students aboard. I don't want to be presumptuous, but that is the kind of pain I feel—a cosmic pain you will do anything to dispel—a 'deep pool of sadness.'

Another way to describe it is as a black metal rod with a flame emanating from it. All you can contemplate is suicide. You don't believe there will ever be morning again. And yet suddenly morning comes. The depression lifts, the sun rises again.

I have a lot of dreams, and I think the tail end of those can sometimes drop me into a dark depression. From the time I was nine I had a recurring dream of walking down a long hallway with a series of closed doors. I was so afraid that beyond those doors was an abyss worse than death. That terror was so enveloping that I finally went to a hypnotist. I had never believed in hypnotism up to that time. I thought it was some kind of trickery, but that therapy got to the bottom of the nightmare.

Under hypnotism I discovered that the dream evolved from a real childhood experience. I don't remember exactly where I was, in some abandoned building, I think, but I was escaping from a sex abuser, who had tried to grab me and pull me into a room. I finally escaped from him, but it wasn't easy and my clothes were torn and dirty. I couldn't have been very old then because my mother was still alive. When I told her of this horrible encounter, all she said was, 'Don't ever tell your father.' So I didn't tell anybody, including myself! In fact, I had completely repressed that memory until the unconscious brought it back. Then I could deal with it and put it away. The amazing thing is that I haven't had that nightmare since.

I was always alone as a child and an adolescent, and I am most comfortable alone even today. But I'm happy when my husband is in the house with me, and I'm most complete then. He has furnished most of the empty rooms of my past. But being alone is a natural state for me."

CHILDHOOD TRAUMAS:
DEEP WOUNDS FOR SHELLEY

Most depressed individuals tend to treat every event in their lives, even insignificant problems, as a calamity and to see the world as a bleak place. This perception becomes part of the depressed person's self-image as a hopeless, worthless individual.

But Shelley's bouts of depression, brought on in all probability by her traumatic childhood, differ from the usual experience in that she is naturally a hopeful, optimistic person, and her depressions are brief in duration—usually no more than twenty-four hours—but of such terrible intensity that the pain is almost unbearable. And although Shelley walks around with a feeling of "great empty spaces" inside, she is a naturally resourceful person with courage and fortitude.

Shelley credits much of her survival to her inborn intelligence. Lewis Terman, creator of the Stanford-Binet IQ tests, made extensive studies of "gifted children" (children with an IQ of 130 or more) and found that these children were not only generally larger and healthier than peers in a control group; they were also more *emotionally adjusted.* The gifted child of nine, he proposed, had reached a level of character development of the average fourteen-year-old! This superiority was found to be even greater among girls than boys.

Although most of the children in the study came from better homes (both in terms of educational level and income), Terman found nothing in their environment that would account to any large extent for the accelerated development of gifted children—or "termites" as these children came to be called. Terman and his colleagues hypothesized, as a result of these findings, that superior development of such youngsters was "in their genes."

Certainly Shelley's outstanding intelligence gave her first passage into the world of the imagination and escape from her own harsh environment. At three she taught herself to read and was a voracious reader from then on. Her library card was her "most valuable possession," and it was her extraordinary intelligence (and the recognition of that potential) that permitted her entry into the private school— the wonderful school that would shape her life and give direction to her ambitions and career.

Despite her remarkable gifts, Shelley has not escaped unscarred from her painful past. As she herself tells us in dramatic terms, she still suffers deep bouts of depression when she fears she won't have the strength and will to emerge from the tight shroud that threatens to strangle her, the "black metal rod" that sears her spirit. Yet, with the help of ongoing therapy and the deeply understanding support of her husband and family, each time she wakes into the light again.

Shelley's story describes to us the extraordinary capacity of the human psyche to endure and triumph. Although still shaped by bitter experiences of childhood, Shelley, under the guidance of a therapist, has reached a highly evolved state of forgiveness and understanding. The struggle has been long and painful and the battle with intense periods of depressions still returns to haunt her. Yet she continues to:

1. Develop her resources to the fullest, using her own special talents and skills for writing and study.
2. Affirm herself through disciplined pursuit of her interests in early English literature, poetry, sociology, and law.
3. Replace feelings of bitterness and resentment with compassion and insight—understanding the experiences that shaped her parents and forgiving them for the pain they have caused her.
4. Keep an emotional balance and perspective through creativity and caring for others—the two traits, according to Erikson, that sustain us throughout life and particularly as we grow into old age.

Praise, praise the patience
of women
who hold in each palm

blown suns of late August
gold core of lakes
scooped by the glacier

tracing the lee wake of angels
they stand in their jeans
their deep thighs

shaking cold fists at the tide.

—"Praise, Praise"

4

Treasure Hunt

That hot July you lay on
a bed of poison ivy
inside a weedy dugout
sheltered by the dunes.
It was your secret spaces that broke
your arms and legs
into hives which blistered
and ran weeping as I
sat by your bed
rubbing the crazy itch
with cold pink calamine.

You were looking for a father,
you said, inside tangled arms
of the blackberry vine,
in sandy caverns polished with
wet mollusk shells.
Hidden between your socks
in the top dresser drawer
you thought you'd find
a code, a map, a message
that would show you
where to search, a treasure hunt.

And though I tried
to become woman-man,
half Odysseus, half Penelope,
I wouldn't do.
My eyes were not the blue

you wanted, father's blue,
I couldn't stand, though I tried,
a taller stance, crease a mitt
into sweaty rivers, catch a ball
with naked fingers.

And your hideaways, what became
of them, your secret spaces.
Stuffed with a blowsy wind,
did their honeyed silences
grow thin, thin
as lies you tell yourself
or as skin, stretched and mended,
barely covers your heart.

—"Treasure Hunt"

Kate, a beautifully groomed brunette, is a graphics designer for a small textiles company. She is talented, successful, and gifted, with a fulfilling marriage and four handsome sons, two of whom will soon reach college age. Then what is missing?

THE FAMILY SCENE: CONFUSION AND DENIAL

Although Kate appears poised and self-confident, she often feels anxious and insecure, always afraid that she may fall at any moment into a deep and dangerous abyss. Her father was a self-centered alcoholic, and the family focused all its energy on denying the chaos at the center of their lives.

"I was always a forthright person," Kate says, "but it didn't matter. I expressed feelings, but Mother negated them or tried to tell me what I should feel or think. That's still true largely. She's always saying, 'I can't believe that you think that. . . . I can't believe you would do that. . . .'

In thinking about it, I turned to anyone who would listen to me. I had the expected role of being 'good,' the 'achiever,' and I wasn't expected to complain or talk about how things really were. I would pick up the slack at home, do what I was supposed to. Outside, I took up my role of the 'family hero' with a vengeance. I think I earned every Girl Scout badge there was. Since I wasn't a natural athlete, I honed myself for those things I did do well. Academically, I hovered between being a B+ and an A- student. This was at a big school in Chicago, so that kind of achievement was pretty impressive.

And even though I didn't believe one whit in God, I was a big worker in the church. I loved the kind of adulation and attention being a super achiever gave me.

The funny thing is that I was fed up with hypocrisy at an early age. I thought it was pretty funny that Mother was asked to teach a class in family relations at her school when our own relationships were such a mess.

All the time I was growing up I felt lonely and left out—that I never got much of my mother's personal attention. In fact, I didn't think she gave me any. She was too busy keeping up appearances. The house was always perfectly clean and all the kids would be packed up with lunches and snacks, and off we would go to the zoo. This was on weekends of course. She was heavily involved with the Girl Scouts and a den mother and what have you. Inside I was screaming, 'Look at me. I need help!'

She never had time to set any guidelines for me or to discuss things that I needed to know. She never said a word to any of us about sexual matters, never even told me about menstruation or went with me to buy a bra. I was so jealous of my friends whose mothers would take them on shopping expeditions, to buy a bra or a slip or a new sweater. Mother never seemed to have any idea how important those things were.

It still makes me furious when people tell even small social lies because I couldn't get Mother to tell the truth and because our whole life was a lie."

As is the usual scenario in an alcoholic family, the picture Kate's family presented to the outside world was one of harmony and love. The five children went to Sunday school every week even though Kate knew neither she nor her parents "believed in God." Her mother, a teacher in a nearby school, was respected by friends and associates, but because of the pressures on her at home, she could be a "witch" in the family circle. The family lived a life of deception that Kate despises—so much so that even now she feels the little "white lies" that we formulate to avoid hurt or embarrassment are degrading and contemptible.

Families give us continuity, roots, a sense of who we are based on traditions, culture, shared rituals. Yet we are often unaware of the unspoken *family rules* that govern our ideas, our behavior, that may fuel anger or depression or loneliness, the spark that can ignite a flame into a conflagration! We establish both major and minor rules. Some are chiefly a matter of style. In one family, for instance, the serving of dinner on Christmas Eve serves a symbolic function of a shared time together. In another family, birthdays are far more important, and include a heaping of presents on the celebrant or a surprise party. Even the way in which presents are opened, carefully and tenderly or quickly and explosively, becomes a part of the ritual. Such minor customs can become permeated with intense feelings out of all proportion to their importance, and any attempt to change the style or the content of the ceremony will be met with anger and resistance because although they are not necessary for survival, ceremonies give families a sense of cohesiveness and of belonging as an historical and family unit.

The family rules thought essential to survival are the ones that will be defended most strongly and stubbornly. These are the rules that determine the family hierarchy, the positions of power, communication, the perceptions and attitudes of the members, the openness to outside influences. In assessing our own family systems, these are questions we need to ask according to Hartman and Laird:

1. Can rules be talked about, or *are there rules about talking about rules?*
2. How is power distributed in the family? Does one person make all the major decisions, or are choices made on a relatively democratic basis?
3. Is there one member heavily involved in resisting any change in the rules?
4. Does power reside in the rules rather than in any one person?
5. What are the shared principles of the family and do they help to keep members from deviating from a set pattern?
6. What is the extent of communication in the family? Can family members talk to each other about problems and issues?
7. Who is included in that communication and who is left out?
8. Does one person speak, feel, or think for others?
9. Is an effort to communicate honestly and openly ridiculed, denied, or ignored?
10. If the behavior of one member is odd or destructive, does it help maintain the system by keeping the focus off the real problem?

The rules of the family are a powerful force, not only because of the emotional energy that goes into keeping them in place, but because they are unseen, unspoken, and unheard! It's almost impossible to grapple with an invisible presence that is never announced, much less discussed, and that may reach back into a past so deeply rooted and entrained that we never question either the seed or the fruit. When we look at the paradigms of our own families, we need to examine not just the symptoms of our interrelationships but the underlying foundations. As Kate's story unfolds, we find that the unspoken rules of the family—*don't speak the truth, never express real feelings, refuse to face the reality of the violent unpredictable behavior of the alcoholic father*—to be a force that disrupted the lives of every member of the family and would eventually lead to unthinkable loss.

MIXING OF THE GENERATIONS

"A lot was expected of me at home. I resented the role that was put on me—as a policeman—getting everybody fed and in bed while Mom went back to school to get her graduate degree," Kate continues. "But that was my responsibility as the oldest child. I was the 'goodie.' It took me years for that label to fade. In fact, I'm still expected to be the 'rescuer' when it comes to a family crisis or an issue that has to be resolved.

There weren't many rules and regulations in our household. I could do pretty much what I wanted to—walk home from the movies late at night, watch TV when I wanted to. I could do things none of my friends were allowed to, and because of that, *I felt my parents didn't love me.* They didn't care enough to make rules or enforce them. Also, because of this, when we hit adolescence and my parents began to set rules—curfews and the like—my brothers and sisters rebelled in a big way. They were into drinking, smoking, staying out late, all kinds of acting out. I was still 'Miss Goodie,' but I rebelled in ways no one was likely to find out about.

There was constant 'grounding,' but no one paid any attention because none of us had any respect for our father. If he made the rule, it was there to be sneered at. I didn't want to cause embarrassment to Mother, but the other kids never complied with anything. They saw this hypocritical behavior that was going on, the mess in the family and the facade we showed to the world—that everything was under control when nothing was."

COALITIONS AND CROSS—GENERATIONAL ALLIANCES CREATE HAVOC

As we've seen with Laura, Amy, and Ellen, coalitions are quick to form in unhealthy family systems, and nowhere are they more pronounced than in the alcoholic family. In Kate's family, she and her four sisters and brothers were all allied with Mother in a coalition that stood at the end of the triangle, far away from the hostile, abusive father. Rivalry also developed between the siblings as they vied for Mother's attention and developed strategies for staying away from their father's taunting, belittling, and unreasonable rages.

Kate, as the oldest child and daughter, was expected to take on the caretaker's role, looking after her younger siblings and putting her finger in the dike whenever the tide threatened to break through! However, Kate, who urgently needed her mother's attention and affection, resented her role as a "little mother"—and still does! Why should she be expected to resolve the family crises? Why was there never enough time in Mother's agenda for time alone with Kate? It was difficult for her as a child to understand that her mother lived a life of mounting stress, trying to cope with the demands of an addictive husband, take care of the needs of five children, and work as a full-time educator.

With younger sisters and brothers born only a few years apart and the family's difficult financial situation, we can surmise that as an infant Kate may not have received the kind of nurturing she needed to form a secure sense of self and a strong sense of separate boundaries. As we've explored in the teachings of Mahler, that first attachment is all-important in the healthy emotional growth of the toddler.

Ainsworth and her colleagues, using a method of measuring the security of attachment called the *strange situation,* devised a laboratory situation where children were separated from the mother, left with a stranger, and then reunited with the mother. These children fell into three psychological categories—*securely attached, insecure/avoidant,* and *insecure/ambivalent.* The securely attached child was shown to be happy when reunited with the mother after separation but not anxious or hostile. The insecure/avoidant child, on the other hand, would avoid contact with the mother when reunited and treated mother and stranger in approximately the same manner. The insecure/ambivalent child was quite upset when separated from the mother and might show anger at the reunion. She resisted being comforted by mother or stranger.

On the basis of Ainsworth's experiments and further research, child psychologists have come up with findings that show the securely attached child is likely to have higher self-esteem, greater empathy, and greater sociability with peers and adults, and to show less aggressive behavior and less dependency than children who don't feel a secure bond with the mother. Erikson's theory of the stages of development also sees secure attachment as a nucleus for the growth of *trust versus mistrust* in our formative stages.

THE RIGID FAMILY SYSTEM
AND THE NEED FOR INTIMACY

A singular dimension in measuring family boundaries is the extent of love and care family members show for each other. The following criteria, developed chiefly by family centered social workers, Ann Hartman and Joan Laird, assess this dimension:

1. Do family members listen with interest to each other?
2. Do they respect attempts toward growth and change?
3. Do they enjoy being together?
4. Do they find satisfaction in each other's experiences?
5. Can they laugh at each other without ridicule or cruelty?
6. Do they show concern for each other's pain?
7. Do they reach out to each other and touch?
8. Do they talk about ideas and concerns together?
9. Can they openly express feelings to each other?
10. Are they willing to make sacrifices for each other?

Kate's rigid family system appears to measure at the lower end of the "caring scale" in the atmosphere fostered by the alcoholic father. "I never thought that Mother really cared about my problems," Kate relates, "or was honest about her own. I wanted—and still want—desperately to feel close to others. I don't feel I respect their boundaries, their right to privacy. This isn't just with close friends either. Even with people I meet in the supermarket line, I feel this urgent need to speak to them, to hear all about them. I know this is inappropriate, but I can't seem to help myself."

Why this compulsive need for intimacy? In Kate's family there were rigid individual boundaries where the emphasis was on independence, competency, and achievement rather than on affection and close bonding. So Kate even now is trying to fill in the missing link of love and security. The family never expressed real feelings and there was a tacit agreement that no member was allowed to. There might be an explosion of the terrible truth, and then the whole family would fall apart! Her father was a stubborn alcoholic who denied his alcoholism to the last.

Even when he wasn't drinking, Kate feels, her father was not a kind, generous person, but was vain, self-centered, and egotistical. Although in his seventies he finally had to give up drinking because of health problems, he never attempted to resolve the problems that were the seeds of his addiction.

One of the conflicts that looms the largest for Kate now is her desire to know "everything about everyone's private lives." If a friend keeps a "secret" from her, some issue that may be deeply personal, she feels crushed. She knows, rationally, that this is an unrealistic expectation, but when she suddenly learns, for example, that a friend has deep-seated marital problems, she feels betrayed because, according to her perceptions, her friend doesn't trust her enough to tell her the full truth.

Yet honesty is not a requisite for keeping friendships close. On the contrary, we have to honor and respect our friends' boundaries—as well as our own. When we insist on knowing the most intimate details of a friend's problems, we step over that invisible boundary line, and we have to take a step or two back to make sure we don't jeopardize our friendships. Kate herself recognizes this dilemma, but it's still difficult for her to reconcile the conflict between feelings and needs.

As we saw earlier, Amy, at the opposite end of the spectrum, finds it difficult and painful to reveal any details of her personal life. She is reluctant to mention even a positive happening, such as landing a coveted job or winning a scholarship. Living in a reserved family atmosphere in which rigid walls sheltered the family secrets, it's easy to become reclusive and isolated. Fortunately, Amy's life has now taken a different direction because of an open, loving relationship with her new husband and growing self assurance in her own capabilities.

PORTRAIT OF THE ALCOHOLIC

"You could never count on my father for anything," Kate says emphatically. "If he was supposed to be somewhere, take you to an appointment, arrive home for dinner, you could count on it—*he wouldn't be there*. He never recognized he was an alcoholic. It was the 'bossy' women in his life he blamed for all his troubles. My maternal grand-father was an alcoholic too, you see. He was an obvious problem drinker even as a young man, but when he was sober, he was loving and kind, and Mother and her sister adored him—in spite of the drinking.

But this meant Mother grew up in a totally secretive family, and she couldn't see the white elephant even when he stepped on her foot or sat in her lap! At any rate, my mother and her sister also grew up to be achievers and very successful women. My mother was a highly respected educator and my aunt held a high-powered job with a big company. These were the two 'bossy women' my father laid his troubles on.

Mother always strongly disapproved of overeating and smoking. These were *moral* issues for her. She thought people smoked strictly to get attention; she had no idea that you could become addicted to smoking—or alcohol for that matter. My father smoked and so did all my brothers and sisters, but I never could. I wanted to, but couldn't bring myself to disappoint Mother. This is how much I wanted her approval.

My father was basically, I think, a pretty terrible person. He was constantly sniping at others and was a full-fledged bigot and a racist. He would mock anyone he could, and my sisters and I like to dig and needle too. We learned from a master. He was unmerciful.

He was a complete egotist. Other women wanted to 'play' with him because he could be very attractive when he tried. My mother would hear reports, 'Maggie is after your husband.' And of course Mother was at home trying to take care of five children, run the household, and work!

Once when she was about to be carted off to the hospital in an ambulance, one of us went rushing out to the tennis court to tell my father, and his response was that 'he had to finish the set.' Another time, on the Fourth of July, another baby was well on the way, even imminent, and it was time to leave the house, but he had to finish watching the ball game!

We always had money problems of course. My father liked to play 'money games.' He made up this myth that 'the rich don't pay their bills.' What made me really furious was the facade that Mother put on for other people and her pretenses to us as well. She 'had no way of not getting pregnant.' Of course she did, but she wouldn't take care of herself, which she wouldn't admit. On the other hand my father in his later years claimed that she had 'made him impotent.' Naturally, it was alcohol that had caused that state, but someone else was always to blame for all his woes!"

BLAMING OTHERS—THE EASY DEFENSE

When our plans don't turn out the way we had hoped, when the situation at home and at work seems to be veering out of control, it's great to have someone or something we can blame! With this handy defense we take the focus off ourselves and reduce our anxiety about our failures. If we don't take personal responsibility for the chaos we've created, we can maintain an illusion of control, at least temporarily—or until the next crisis looms.

Kate's father, in the typical alcoholic pattern, became an expert at blaming Kate's mother and even her sister for the suffering and destruction he himself had created. According to family therapists, Merle Fossum and Marilyn Mason, a handy rule for pathological families is: *If things don't go the way you planned, blame someone!* When we refuse to recognize that we are responsible for our own actions, we never have to face the human being we see in the mirror every day or the pain we have caused others.

ISOLATION AND LONELINESS:
THE ALCOHOLIC FAMILY LEGACY

"I could bring friends home if I wanted to," Kate says, shaking her dark head. "I did, although not very often. I don't know why I didn't worry that my father might appear drunk and ridiculous at any moment, but maybe it was because he was seldom home. And if he did come in, he would probably sail right out again on some pretense or another. I remember that I did love baby-sitting to get away from the home scene. I was always looking for an invitation to spend the night with a friend, a place where parents doted on their children instead of ridiculing them and giving them orders—'Sit up straight. . . . Put your napkin in your lap. . . . Eat everything on your plate'—these were the kinds of directives we were used to hearing—and worse.

Mother didn't feel she could have friends over because she didn't know what my father might do. However, she did try for a while to invite couples to our house for a casserole and a salad because the cocktail parties they went to could be disastrous. Father would never leave and would get very drunk. Of course he got equally as drunk at his own parties.

Then, too, there was the question of money. The other couples would want to go out for dinner or a snack, and she never felt they could afford to. Later on, when his drinking got progressively worse, I used to feel so bad because I saw they were being left out of their accustomed social life. There were three couples who did everything together, and because of my father's behavior, I'm sure, my parents stopped being included in parties and outings. I still feel hurt over this even though I can understand it.

Father was slim and incredibly handsome for years. He started putting on weight, according to him, when he stopped playing tennis, but I think it was when he lost his job and took on a sales job that allowed him too much free time.

After the sales job began, things went from bad to worse. He was mostly emotionally abusive, although I think he did become physically abusive to Mother later on after I left home. When F. and I were first married, I used to come home for short visits, and it was horrible.

As children, we all had our ways of escaping. We would pretend to be asleep when we heard my father coming in loaded and singing over and over again, 'Son of a Gun from Flint.' Those repetitive songs of his were a sure sign he was in his cups. Mother would lock herself in the bathroom, and we would retreat to our bedrooms. It was pretty scary for all of us."

INVASIONS: THE ADDICT IS AN EXPERT

Let's consider the boundary invasions Kate was subjected to. First, she was the victim of her father's emotional abuse—his constant sarcasm, belittling, and blaming. He was gifted with a sharp and biting tongue that made his children doubt their own achievements whatever they attempted, whether it was skill at tennis or proficiency in cooking or scholarly endeavors. As often happens with insecure egos, he was, in all likelihood, jealous of his own children. His own self-esteem needed constant propping up at the expense of their (and Mother's) self-image.

Second, Kate was bound up in a *cross-generational coalition* that made her the target of family anxiety and forced her into becoming the family savior—the achiever at school, in the church, and in the community who, by dint of good deeds and honors at school, would keep the family name intact. Of course this was an impossible task as well as a fruitless one. Despite her Herculean efforts, she couldn't hide the family's secrets. No matter what we do, shameful secrets have a way of seeping out, and everyone knows Father is a drinker, carouser, reckless driver, or a volatile tennis partner. The only persons we protect from the truth are ourselves.

To add insult to injury, Kate herself, always the caretaker, the "little mother," longed for loving attention. When she attempted to express her very real feelings of anger or sadness or frustration, she was rebuffed with denial and sometimes began to doubt her own hold on reality. The family's position in the social hierarchy was always precarious, and Kate somehow felt responsible even for that—if only she were more clever and tenacious, maybe she could make up for all the family losses!

MODELING: WE IMITATE WHAT WE KNOW

Bandura suggests that children learn behavior chiefly through *modeling*—by watching how others react and behave. The child who watches her parents show generosity or consideration to a neighbor or friend will learn to be giving and thoughtful. The child who sees her parents resolve problems through temper tantrums and respond to conflict with anger and violence, will learn aggression and violence as a way of solving problems. Research also indicates that when there is a difference between what the model says and what he does, *we imitate the doing, not the saying*.

Of course there are other more complex factors that influence the child's development such as temperament and mitigating influences of a teacher or relative or family friend. And we have to factor in as well the compound variables that affect the equation. A child who sees violence and aggression in the home is often also the target of irrational anger and possibly physical and emotional abuse and may react by withdrawal and isolation rather than hostility.

In Kate's home each of the children learned one lesson well: don't be like Father! They have all seen the misery he instigated when he broke his promises or lashed out at his children and wife with irrational anger. And yet the pathological chain has an insidious way of perpetuating itself—*we are angry because we have been treated with contempt and indifference. We are fearful because we haven't learned a sure sense of who we are. We are anxious because we have never gotten the attention we need. We are demanding and intolerant with our children because this is what we know!*

THE ACCIDENT: CHAOS AND LOSS

"My mother couldn't leave my father," Kate says, "because he had her convinced she would lose everything if she did. When we (my brothers, sisters, and I) begged her to leave him, she was sure that, through some smart lawyer he knew, he would manage to keep the house, the antiques, everything she had scraped and saved to pay for. Her salary had paid for a lot through the years, but she would end up with nothing and be totally poverty-stricken. And that could have been the case.

My brother, David, was a genius of some sort, I think, but very rebellious. He graduated from high school with probably a 'C' average because he didn't care. Mother applied for him at the university and since his test scores were so high, the school said they would accept him, but not for another year. Then, when he did get there, they wanted him to take basic math, statistics and the like, and he refused. So he was pretty much at loose ends at eighteen and looking for trouble.

For instance, he was put in jail once because of using a false ID to buy drinks. I think he must have been an alcoholic. He was sullen, never showed emotion. Then he had a terrible automobile accident when he was eighteen, probably drinking and driving. He lost the use of both arms and legs and was competely helpless. Mother was really trapped at that point.

My father couldn't let go of the idea that David was going to be everything he hadn't been, and the accident exacerbated a situation that was already awful. After the accident, when he lost the use of both arms and legs, he was very manipulative with Mother. Because he had to have sleeping pills in order to overcome the pain and to sleep, he would have Mother up half the night doling them out to him. He couldn't even take a pill on his own, you see.

This started to interfere with her professional life because she got hooked on sleeping pills too—never sleeping and living with so much anxiety and stress. She managed to get herself off these when she realized what was happening, but then I think she started to drink too much herself. It was a defense against Father's drinking and an escape from the misery her life had become, I'm sure.

My youngest brother, Craig, got out as soon as he could and moved into his own place; he couldn't take it. And Mother couldn't leave the state because she needed the benefits from her teaching job. There was no way she could leave either David or my father at that point.

Also she still felt he (David) was redeemable. He hadn't lost his brain power at all, and she was convinced that he could learn to use a computer and make some use of his life. He was in various rehab centers, and professionals as well as friends took heroic measures to try to get him involved in something on the outside. But he wouldn't try. Basically, he just gave up and finally, twelve years after the accident, committed suicide when Mother was away. He had saved up pills for a long time, a big enough dose to kill himself.

Although I was married and living away from home at the time, this was a loss that none of us in the family could ignore. We all suffered the pain and sorrow of his suicide, and yet at the same time I felt a kind of anger at my brother for imposing this kind of burden on us."

Kate's story could be a narrative from Greek tragedy, where all the Furies strike at once. Her father's drinking and destructive behavior grew progressively more uncontrollable, the adolescent children flaunted the parents' rules, becoming more and more rebellious, and finally Kate's brother, David, became a hopeless cripple in an automobile accident.

This family had few, if any, coping skills. They had never learned how to communicate with each other, give each other sustenance and love, encourage and console one another so that in times of crisis, despair deepened and intensified. Kate's mother tried desperately to redeem her son's life, but in the end, there was little anyone could do but endure.

KATE'S ISOLATION HEIGHTENS

"Even when my first son was born, my parents couldn't come down from their vacation cottage to be with me," Kate says. "On the other hand, my husband's mother flew over from Europe to help us out!

Maybe one of the reasons control is an important issue to me is that things never were under control in our house. I have to reassure myself on every occasion that things are not going to fall apart when I lose control. I'm agitated and unhappy at first and have to really work at it to get my perspective back. It's also hard for me to accept that everyone doesn't like me, that they don't have to.

And I want to make every occasion really special and perfect. If I'm not in control, I know it won't be perfection to the nth degree. Maybe this is because I feel there was never anything special for me as a child, and I'm going to be sure I make up for it from now on."

CONTROL: WHY DO WE NEED IT?

Melody Beattie suggests that many of us—especially as daughters and sons of alcoholics—feel that we can keep the world circling in orbit by sheer force of will and mental energy. But we find when we do let go, the world keeps whirling around the same as ever, the grass continues to grow, the seasons change. And we discover to our surprise that the universe will not dissolve into chaos the moment we look away and relinquish control.

This kind of thinking begins in childhood with believing and praying that if only we are clever enough, if we attend to every detail, morning, evening, and night, we can somehow stop the alcoholic from drinking. We try prayer, magic spells, and voodoo, but nothing works. And though experience proves us wrong every time, we only try harder!

Control is only an illusion and the strange part, according to the insights that Beattie gives us, is that *what we attempt to control—other people's behavior, events in our lives, addiction—ends up controlling us. In fact, the only aspect of our lives we can control is our own behavior.* Perhaps that is the tallest order of all.

Perfectionism is a part of control and implies the same kind of magical thinking—if I wash every window, arrange every flower, and wind every clock, then nothing can possibly happen to the wonder of the occasion, the happiness of my home. But perfectionism, as a handmaiden of control, also ends up controlling us—we are bound to the slavery of being perfect, allowing for no flaws in the facade, and this is an exhausting and frustrating task. Our labors never end because perfectionism is obsessive and Utopia keeps slipping away just as we think we've attained the ideal state.

BOUNDARY SETTING: THE STEPS FOR KATE

What has Kate done—what can she do now—to keep her life manageable? As Kate herself asserts, the process of recovery from a painful childhood goes on every hour, every day, and you can't expect miracles overnight. But working with a therapist to keep her perspective in balance, these are the steps she recommends:

1. Resolve your feelings of bitterness and hurt from the past. Even if you can't forgive a parent for the damage to your life, you can accept those feelings as valid and then let them go.
2. Accept the uncertainty and unpredictability of events and circumstances. And begin by recognizing that the need for control is self-defeating.
3. Affirm your own worth and talents by recognizing the positive in yourself and letting go of the negative. (Incidentally, this same attitude of praise and encouragement toward family and friends not only empowers them, but also gives power to our own lives.)
4. Enlist the support and caring compassion of others through twelve-step programs like AA, Al-Anon, and ACOA (Adult Children of Alcoholics).

PARALLEL LIVES?

At first glance, Kate and Barbara appear to have little in common. They live very different lifestyles and in very different geographic areas—Kate in the Northwest, Barbara on an island off the coast of Florida. But looking beneath the surface, we find distinctive parallels. Both Kate and Barbara grew up in families with rigid boundaries, leaving them with a precarious sense of self. Both family systems found it difficult to express affection and lacked communication or flexibility. Denial and deception were the unspoken rules that governed the family conduct. Yet Kate and Barbara are naturally open and direct and have a hard time holding back whatever they are feeling or thinking.

Vivacious and articulate, Barbara works part-time as a waitress in an upscale restaurant, but the real Barbara is an artist who writes poetry and articles for a local paper. When I first met her, I was struck with her air of confidence and warmth. Although we had met on a casual basis, I soon felt free to talk openly with her about poetry, art, religion, and relationships.

When I learned of her troubled childhood, I was impressed even more with the aura of serenity that is the basis of Barbara's personality. Yet she still has to struggle to maintain a strong sense of self, to recognize that the person she is today is insightful, imaginative, and a survivor! For the struggle has never been easy or smooth since the day she entered the world, the daughter of an adolescent who was still a child herself.

A STORY OF EMOTIONAL HARDSHIP
AND PHYSICAL ABUSE

Barbara's relationship with her child-mother has always been—and is still—one of ambivalence, of admiration mixed with shame, love with disappointment. Barbara says:

"My mother has been embarrassed by me from day one. Ever since I was a little girl I was outspoken, would say anything. At Sunday school, for example, I claimed to have been found in the bulrushes like Moses. I was kicked out of Sunday school for that. Can you imagine it? I never could keep secrets, and my mother was just the opposite. She never wanted anyone to know anything about what was going on in the family.

To understand my background at all, you have to know that my mother was only sixteen when I was born. And she was never married to my real father, who was already a married man and who died a few years later at age twenty-seven in a mining accident. When she found out she was pregnant, she married someone else. This man turned out to be a brute, and that was a disaster. It was so hard for her. I had to go into a foster home when I was three.

The foster home was a traumatic experience for me. I was beaten every day and treated terribly in every way. They even tied me up and hung me in a burlap bag. It was unbelievably bad. This lasted about six months of my life, but it has taken me the rest of my life to get over it. I think I finally am now. My faith and my religion have helped me keep my sanity—helped me cope with being a damaged person. And my husband, who is the most understanding person alive.

Another tragedy occurred the year I was two or three. My stepfather came and carried my little brother off. He was about sixteen months old at the time, and I had no understanding of why he had to leave. We had different fathers, but I didn't know that. I was heartbroken.

Mother has dropped a veil over all that. It's as if it never happened. She and I have weathered a lot of storms, not all of them too successfully."

ABUSE AND LOSS: THE EARLY YEARS

If Kate's story is a Greek tragedy, Barbara's is a novel, one that is scarcely credible in the twentieth century. It's a story out of Charles Dickens, a tale in which children are abused by their keepers, starved, neglected, beaten, and, in Barbara's case, "tied and hung in a burlap bag" by her foster family—an experience of such horror that even now it's difficult for her to recall it.

Fortunately, she was soon rescued from this abusive setting, but another trauma was to follow—the disappearance of her baby brother, whom she loved dearly. And Barbara's mother, still a child when her daughter was born, would never develop into the kind of compassionate, nurturing person who could give her child the security she needed. Just as with Kate, Barbara would begin a lifelong search for the affection and nurturance missing from her childhood.

In his studies of infants and young children, Bowlby emphasize the need for a physical attachment to one object or person. He feels that if this primitive need is denied, then the result will be apathy and a turning away from society. Bowlby suggests that this basic need even extends to animals and is more than a matter of simply being fed and protected, that all of us must have secure and loving attachments if we are to develop into secure adults. Individuals who don't have this kind of support are extremely vulnerable to any kind of stress and may become overdependent in all their relationships.

Mahler extended this theory to include the process of separation and individuation in the development process. The good mother reassures and comforts the baby by feeding, changing, holding, and taking care of all her needs. The young child, with a high sense of security and attachment, is able to separate from the mother and become a well-integrated personality. On the other hand, the failure to separate from the mother (or caregiver) results in overdependence on the family and handicaps the person's ability to meet challenges in the outside world.

THE POWER OF THE WEAK

"When I was five years old," Barbara states, "my mother married a man from a sprawling Italian family. He was kind to me, and I loved him as a child.

As I've said, Mother and I had an ambivalent relationship. I was a projection of her, I think, although we were totally different. She used to coax my hair into long curls and wanted me to wear the prettiest dresses. On the other hand, she would allow me to hurt myself. Once I found an old razor in a tin box. I asked her if this could cut me. She said that it would and when I didn't appear to believe her, she let me go ahead and try it. It really hurt."

Although we want our children to be self-sufficient and to learn by trial and error, we have to make rules to protect them. We can't let a toddler put his hand on the blistering hot coals to find out that they burn! And we show our love by teaching children rules that both protect and encourage self-discipline.

Barbara's mother, Jennie, was childish and ego-centered, anything but disciplined in her emotions. She constantly threatened to disrupt or even destroy the family with (unspoken) implications of abandonment and suicide. Barbara, her stepfather, and her brother were all afraid that if they failed to meet the mother's demands, she would automatically destroy herself, carrying them all down with her to inevitable doom. Barbara dramatizes the flagrant behavior of her mother in a moving narrative lyric.

> My mother liked swimming after sunset,
> she liked moonless nights best.
> Summer nights we walked down to the lake,
> my mom, my dad, the baby in a stroller, and me.
> Although I was only four
> I still remember clearly the aching fear
>
> when my mother slipped into the water.
> She never made a sound as she swam away
> so I listened to my brother's breathing
> and looked for stars in the still soft night
> as my mother swam farther and farther
>
> away, to where we couldn't see her anymore.
> She swam way off to the middle of the lake
> and then she swam back to the shore.
> She'd emerge from the water proud and tall
> like a Venus being born.
> Swimming always made her feel better
> at least for a little while.
>
> She'd shake her head and dry her hair
> and when she saw my tears, she'd laugh at me
> she'd say I was 'silly' or 'damned foolish.'

But I could never stop being scared when she
disappeared like a fish into that inky silence.
As the night blotted blues and pinks from the sky,

I'd stand at the end, too nervous to sit
next to my brother who didn't care about anything.
My dad smoked cigarettes and searched for flat stones
to skim over the greenblack surface of the water.
I remember waiting there, shivering in the dark,
my shame as scary and bottomless as the lake,
hoping that the night would give her back to us,
hoping almost that it wouldn't.

—"At the Lake" by Barbara

This powerful poem conveys an eerie sense of the dark beauty of
the lake, its strong undercurrents, the helpless child watching as her
mother threatened to undermine the outwardly peaceful collage of
the small family. Barbara observed her mother's display of power, fas-
cinated yet terrified that she would (or would not) emerge from the
"greenblack surface of the water." Although Barbara's story is told
from an adult perspective, we sense that even the four-year-old felt
the terrible ambivalence of love and hate as she witnessed the conflict between life and death, hope and loss. Clearly the pathological
mother maintains her position of power by playing on the emotions
of those who loved her.

It is a paradox that often the weakest, most pathological member
of the family becomes the central core of the family system. How do
these weak, dependent people become so powerful? Simply because
the family system is always resisting change, even positive change, the
family will go to any lengths to protect the neurotic or abusive member. They will deny, project, rationalize, repress—using every defense
mechanism we can name—to hold the family together and protect it
from outside criticism and even ostracism.

Defense mechanisms come into play when conflicts emerge with
warring elements in the personality and we don't know how to handle
the ensuing anxiety. These are automatic, unconscious responses that
we are not aware of, and often they are necessary to protect us from
pain that the psyche can't handle at the time. Barbara, for example,
has enormous blanks in her childhood, experiences that have been
repressed so deeply that she remembers nothing of them. A child

who is sexually abused (as we'll see with Marie in the next chapter) will often repress her strong feelings of guilt, sadness, and shame. Repression is necessary in the beginning to protect us from the terrible pain and sometimes guilt or shame we feel when we are abused, but if we continue to use defenses to protect us from reality, we stay out of touch with feelings that lie buried but smoldering inside of us.

When we talk about how a single pathological person can take control of the interworkings of the family, we come to the question of power, which Haley believes to be central to all human relationships. Within the family system individuals organize themselves into unequal positions of dominance and submission. Although the family is a world of circular interactions with one action feeding upon the other, it's clear that we still occupy positions of varying status. And although in the case of Amy, Ellen, and Barbara, a neurotic mother dominates the family, the father, the traditional breadwinner and patriarch, often assumes the chief position of power.

If we, as fathers or mothers or grandfathers or grandmothers, overuse our power, we do violence to ourselves and others. There is no such thing as a "benevolent dictatorship" since power corrupts. Even a little power granted to the police officer on the beat or the teacher in the classroom can convey the illusion that they are gods and omnipotent. And absolute power in the hands of one, or several, corrupts nations and individuals.

THE TURNING

"I have some enormous blanks in my childhood," Barbara says thoughtfully. "I remember my brother being born and that I loved him. And I know that from the time I was three years old, I was a voracious reader. My grandfather would point out words in the paper to me, and I learned to read from that experience. Books were important to my mother too. She loved fairytales and gave me generous helpings of myths, fairytales, Aesop's Fables. I can't really remember her reading them to me, but I know she must have.

And I remember my childhood friend, Anita, who was black. I was very sad when I first started school, and it was wonderful that Anita was in the same 'smart' group with me. I had already read a lot by the time I started school so that gave me a good boost in the beginning. Because Anita was black and an outcast as well, I immediately identified with her, probably because I always felt like one of society's outcasts too.

Her mother, Esther, was terrific for me. The family would take me with them to New York City on family trips, and I stayed overnight with them a lot. I went from never having seen a black person to seeing a whole family almost constantly. I didn't ever develop any prejudices. I had a deep love and respect for Esther. She could cook and did—wonderful meals. And she loved me in return. I never had known much nurturing, and this was a new experience. She cared about everything I did or felt.

My mother was not a nurturing person to me. She doesn't touch. I had to learn to, but we didn't do that in my family. Now I think that this is all there is, loving each other, helping each other, sharing, making each other happy."

The appearance of Anita and her family in Barbara's life was something of a miracle. Barbara sensed at once that Anita, as one of the few blacks in her suburban school, was also an outcast, and this formed an immediate bond between the two sensitive young girls. But Anita was also smart and talented and, unlike Barbara, belonged to a close-knit affectionate family. At last Barbara could feel like a loved member of a family who talked with each other, had meals and outings together, laughed and played together. In this setting Barbara would begin the slow process of healing, believing that she was a worthwhile person who was both lovable and capable. But there were still troubles ahead!

INVASIONS AND MORE

"My stepfather, probably without ever recognizing it," Barbara says candidly, "became sexually abusive when I was in my teens. It wasn't overt, but he discussed my clothes with me, would make suggestive remarks. I found out about sex from the men's magazines he left lying around. He read a lot of semipornography—cartoon illustrations and stories of unapproachable women who would have insatiable sex with rough men. That sort of thing.

Mother did not respect my privacy. She would go through my papers and letters. I was a great letter writer. I had a lot of boyfriends in high school, and she would read my letters to them. Everything was hers. Later she would go through her lovers' boxes and papers too—the ones that lived with us.

I wasn't allowed to close doors either. Even now she pounds on my door when I visit her. I never feel comfortable with her because she hasn't changed.

She didn't give me much encouragement either toward being an artistic, creative person or pursuing the things that interested me. She wanted me to work for the telephone company or become a schoolteacher because of the benefits.

How I looked was very important to her, all the superficial things. She was terribly concerned with appearances. Once when I was around sixteen years old, I made a suicide attempt, took most of a bottle of aspirin. She wasn't concerned about *me* when this happened, my state of mind, what had prompted me to do such a thing. All she worried about was *what would people think of her?*

INVASIONS—WILL THEY EVER END?

Barbara's life, from the moment of her traumatic birth, has consisted of invasions—physical and emotional abuse from her foster family, separation from her mother, a lack of support and nurturance during the years of her childhood. During adolescence she experienced covert sexual invasions from her stepfather, who began to see her as a sex object, making suggestive remarks to her and leaving pornographic magazines prominently displayed in the household.

Her mother had little respect for her daughter's privacy or inner life. She pried into everything, never allowing her to maintain a "closed door" on her relationships with her boyfriends or her thoughts or feelings. How many times have we seen this invasion of privacy with unhealthy families? With Laura, Ellen, Amy, and now Barbara! Parents in such families can't allow their children the healthy boundaries they need to protect their inner lives because they, the parents, are too afraid—afraid of losing control over their children's lives, afraid their children will grow up and abandon them.

As Barbara's history illustrates, her mother was never a giving, caring person. Wrapped up in her own needs, she was chiefly concerned with appearances. She worried about her daughter's future only in terms of what would bring financial security, not her dreams or ambitions. And she had no coping resources—no sources of inner strength or insight—for dealing with the series of crises that began with her own unwanted pregnancy.

Even when Barbara made a serious attempt at suicide at age six-teen, her mother was afraid to look below the surface for the causes of her daughter's suffering. She never asked what was missing in the life of this popular, attractive young daughter that she would want to take her own life or what could be done to strengthen and sustain her. She cared only that neighbors and friends might discover her resounding failure as a mother.

USING YOUR POWER

"Because of my mother's attitude and a lot of other factors—wanting attention and power probably—I became extremely sexually promis-cuous in adolescence," Barbara says quietly. "I discovered I had tre-mendous power. I said then that I hated men, but I think now this was an expression of anger at my mother and myself, how I used men to get what I wanted. I would say now men are like children. You have to coax them along. With the exception of my current husband, who is very evolved.

With my first husband it was mainly lust for each other. He was Spanish and quite rigid. We had a beautiful son together who seems very healthy. It's amazing. My first husband has put himself together since then. We have an amicable relationship now. Partly because I've put myself together too.

My son lives with his father. Because of my own upbringing—or lack of it—I was afraid to raise my own child. Living with my mother made me doubt my own capability. She always pooh-poohed every-thing about me and still does. She doesn't like my hair or the way I dress. I didn't develop much of a sense of self. But I see my son every weekend and talk to him all the time. We're very close.

I just learned recently from my mother who my real father was. She finally broke down and told me after all these years. And then, in a kind of amazing coincidence, I stumbled on my father's family on a trip to Ontario. Actually I called them once I knew his name and the city where he was brought up. I was able to trace my roots back to the family name, and I made a trip there.

I was a little afraid of meeting the family like that—an unknown, unacknowledged daughter whom even their son never knew. But they are a boisterous, outgoing lot and welcomed me into the family strong-hold. That gave me a great sense of belonging, of putting my roots down with a real family at last.

But my mother has 'dropped a veil' over the tragedies in her life. Otherwise she believes she couldn't bear the pain and frustration of it. She might be a lot healthier if she could come to terms with it. But I don't think she ever will."

Barbara very early blossomed into a gregarious young woman who was attractive to men. This was her first taste of power, and once she realized the control it gave her, she began to use it. She was, in her own words, "sexually promiscuous" and yet contemptuous of the men she attracted. She had numerous boyfriends, dates, and affairs, and yet because she had never resolved her own feelings of inadequacy, these relationships brought her little lasting happiness. And her relationship with her first husband, based almost entirely on physical attraction (or, as she so succinctly deems it, "lust"), was doomed to failure because of his patriarchal unyielding Spanish heritage.

As we examine Barbara's unfolding story, we begin to see her evolution into the compassionate person she is today.

SETTING LIMITS

"I wrestle with the problem daily of setting boundaries. I don't think I have any—or not enough anyway. As a waitress I have a hard time because of working with homosexuals. Why homosexuals? Because they are sensitive and yet can be demanding too.

Just to give you a small example, everyone always comes to me for change, and I end up giving away a lot of quarters because it's hard to keep track. At the end of the week it's probably cost me about $5.00. That's not a lot, but it's characteristic of how I handle things in general. It's difficult for me to say, 'Keep away, this is my space.' And because I laugh and joke, people will tell me that I'm a 'card' or refuse to take me seriously when I do get angry. Working with a bunch of men—especially sensitive, artistic men—is frustrating.

I have a good marriage. We've negotiated our boundaries in our marriage well, I think. We both believe in giving each other space and flexibility for what we want to do. Of course we are still negotiating—that never stops. But my husband, as I've said, is the most evolved person I know. He has the best of all the masculine and feminine characteristics, strength with sensitivity. He's a musician so he understands the creative impulse and the longing to transcend the ordinary.

I'm happy that I'm using some of my creative talents too—writing a humor column once a week for the local paper. And now the *Gazette* has suggested they are interested in picking my column up. I'm writing a lot of poetry as well.

What has sustained me all along is that I always recognized something special in myself that wasn't available to other mortals. People met me and liked me—still do. There was a light that shone inside me. I was born with faith. That part of me was God.

My parents didn't go to church but I did, and the church taught me to sing. This was a joyful thing for me, being in God's house. In the years since my spirituality has become more defined. What I believe is that God is a river that touches all of us and gives us great solace."

SECRETS OF A SURVIVOR: BARBARA'S STORY

Barbara would tell you emphatically that the key to her survival is no secret! It's been a long, painful journey through the wilderness, coping with early physical and emotional trauma; changes in her lifestyle as her mother moved through marriages, divorce, and separation; emotional deprivation with an immature ego-centered mother; covert sexual harassment from a stepfather; and her own unsettling experiences as she developed into a young woman.

But she is coming into her own. Although she still struggles with setting limits in her relationships with co-workers and friends, she has a good marriage to a man she respects and loves deeply, her relationship with her son is close and loving, she has just published a collection of her essays, and has achieved a degree of serenity that seems amazing in view of her painful background. These are the steps that have been most positive for Barbara as she comes into her own at last. She is learning to:

1. Assert herself when she feels others are taking advantage of her and to speak out clearly and directly—without being cruel.
2. Resolve her feelings toward her mother. She doesn't have to forgive her (we can't always forgive!), but in order to let go of resentment at her painful past, she has to accept her own feelings and let them go.
3. Build self-esteem through exploring, learning, and using her creative talents to the fullest.
4. Continue to build her relationship with her husband and son through setting and negotiating issues, communicating with them on a deep level, and showing love and affection in actions as well as words.

BREAKING THE CHAIN: IT ONLY TAKES ONE GENERATION!

In the *triangulation process* tension between a husband and wife is deflected, though not resolved, by passing it on to a child, which leads to an overly intense and dependent attachment between parent and child. The child's functioning is then crippled, and the mother is able to exert a high degree of control over a daughter's or son's behavior. Such a child, as we've discovered, develops a low level of *differentiation of self.*

But when the undifferentiated child grows up and establishes her own marital relationship, she brings with her the unresolved problems and immaturity from the family of origin. To complicate the issue further, individuals often seek out partners with a similar level of dependency or fusion, so that there may be distancing between husband and wife, physical or emotional dysfunction in either partner, overt conflict between the two partners, or transference of the problem to one or more of the children.

Then the process of triangulation begins again in the *multigenerational transmission process.* Until the link is broken, the chain of emotional illness is passed on from one generation to the next, growing progressively worse with each succeeding generation! Fortunately for all of us, the pattern of multigenerational transmission, in which the family emotional process is passed on through the generations, is not just a negative principle that indicates a future of downward spirals. We not only pass our weaknesses on from one generation to another, we also pass on our strengths! Thus the family with a high level of communication and flexibility, a family that encourages independence and separation, leaves its heritage of health and emotional balance to its sons and daughters. And the child of this generation usually emerges with an even higher level of independence and, in turn, passes self-reliance, high self-esteem, generosity, and compassion for others on to her children. This is why we have families who are known for decades for their outstanding achievements and standards—or for the lack of them.

And when we have daughters like Barbara, who break the chain of pathology, we begin a new cycle illumined by "the light that shines inside."

> From her kitchen window
> she tossed the shining beans

and watched to her surprise
a vine spring up, a leafy vine,
blue flowers.
Calmly she called her son,
her daughter napping
by the cat's slow path.
She followed last embracing
the great tendrils
to catch them if they fell,
her daughter and her son,
but they were used to slippery footholds,
wind that left you gasping
with a rush of sweet manure.
The rest, the rest was easy,
changing breath to breathing,
stone to plum.

—"A Twentieth Century Tale of the Beanstalk"

5

A Burning Barrow

In my quiet bed I lie,
lie for hours
while stars brood,
the moon aches,
my brain thunders
and the trees
forget their splendor,
rusty leaves dissolving
in cold fields.

I wheel a burning barrow
of ghosts onto the lawn.
Ghosts, I burn them nightly,
nightly they rise again
to whimper with
the wounded moon,
each blinded star.

—"A Burning Barrow"

A slight brunette with sad, blue eyes, Marie radiates an air of innocence and fragility that makes everyone she meets want to comfort
and protect her. A young woman still in her early twenties, she suffered long-term sexual abuse from her father—with the unspoken
but very real collusion, if not active encouragement, of her mother, a
cold, controlling woman who hates all physical contact.

Marie says calmly, without apparent emotion, "I was sexually violated as a child by my father and later by a brother as well. It started
so early with my father, who was a violent alcoholic, that whole periods of my childhood are gone—completely erased as if they had never
happened. I can't remember a bout with measles at age nine or learning to ice skate that same winter. A cousin reminded me not long ago
of so much I've forgotten. For a long time now I've been working
with a therapist, trying to recover from all the trauma and bring my
childhood back, but there are chapters I'll never know. Whole chapters. I must have repressed everything."

SEXUAL ABUSE: THE DARK INVASION

What does abuse have to do with boundaries? A great deal, it seems.
According to the experts, *any type of abuse, physical, emotional, or sexual,
is a boundary invasion.* Abusive fathers, mothers, husbands, and lovers don't respect privacy, rights or feelings. To fill vacancies in their
own needy egos, they greedily devour the child's (or spouse's) inner
self. Victims of long-lasting abuse have no strong sense of self, no
idea of how to form caring, intimate relationships because their closest relationships have generated only anger and pain, and they grow
up feeling lonely, isolated, and shamed. Such families lack clear and
flexible boundaries that encourage respect for others and permit
communication between family members, and they, like the children
of alcoholics, are all bound together in a shameful and guilt-ridden
system.

Clinical evidence clearly demonstrates that sexually abusive families are strongly *enmeshed,* with *weak individual boundaries* and a *high
degree of dependency* between family members. There is no clear separation between the generations or between sisters and brothers although such bonds may be angry, conflicting ones. However, these
families build *rigid external boundaries* between themselves and society,
and powerful external boundaries isolate the family from the community and protect the shamed family system from threat of change
and outside influence. When one member threatens to break out of
this well-fortified enclosure and reveal the family secrets, the walls
grow higher and the remaining members are bound even more tightly
together.

Of all the forms of abuse, sexual abuse is the most flagrant violation of boundaries because, as psychologists Mary Jo Barret and Terry

Trepper suggest, it violates basic trust between parent and child. This category of abuse usually connotes an unspoken collusion between mother and father so that the implications are especially disturbing. In such a scenario the father perpetrates the abuse and the mother tolerates it either out of fear or ambivalent sexual feelings on her own part. When this is the case, how can the child possibly trust anyone? Certainly she can't trust her own parents who profess to love and care for her. Thus she grows up believing that the world is a deceitful place, and she can't put her faith in anyone. Marie describes that frightening world succinctly.

MARIE'S STORY: ABUSE AND DENIAL

"I was terrified of my father and sickened at the same time," Marie states, her eyes welling with tears. "I never knew when he might come creeping up after dark—I thought of him as a monster with long, hairy tentacles reaching out to grab me. He could be violent if I tried to resist. He was usually drunk. Sometimes his sloppy affection would turn to anger, and he would kick or slap me. He even tried to seduce one of my friends once so I never, ever had friends stay over at my house again after that.

My parents wouldn't allow me to lock the bedroom door, and I lived in terror of my father's shadowy visits. I don't like to think of him as *my father*, actually. That's just a biological accident that doesn't count for a thing."

ALCOHOL AND ABUSE:
TWIN BROTHERS OF PATHOLOGY

When we consider that in a high percentage of child abuse cases, alcohol or drugs is a dominant factor and that one in three families reports alcohol abuse by a family member, the role that drug addiction plays in abusive situations can scarcely be overplayed. And alcoholism and abuse, twin brothers of violence and pathology, are great enforcers of the *family myth*. The family myth describes the family as a harmonious group with endless potential—except for one member, who always causes problems. This member is usually one child (or more), the *scapegoat*, who is made responsible for all the family's misery. The scapegoat not only has to live with conflict and chaos; she is the focus of the family's anger and has to bear the burden of all their failures. It's not surprising, then, that there is a strong correlation between incest and adolescent drug addiction. Some rehabilitation centers for adolescent drug and alcohol users report that a startling 75 percent of their patients are *incest victims.*

Marie's experience represents a reckless violation of individual boundaries not only by the father but also by the entire family. Every member of the family enables the abuser by protecting him and keeping silent—burying the shameful family secret as deeply as possible. Marie, forced at age five into sexual activities with an adult male, a frightening figure of giant proportions, could easily have been crushed except for her remarkably strong spirit. Instinctively she knew that this furtive relationship was wrong and shameful, but no one appeared to notice, not even her own mother. In fact, Marie was certain something must be terribly wrong *with her* because her reality bore little or no resemblance to the family facade of propriety. It must be that she was the difficult one and had only herself to blame for some mysterious quality that fostered this unhealthy act.

"No one challenged my father or spoke up to him," Marie relates. "Not that anyone had any affection or respect for him except for a healthy respect for his violent temper. He kept us all intimidated with his reign of terror—breaking things, kicking down doors, the whole bit."

A TWISTED TALE

The dark ethos of physical violation grows even darker when we consider that sexual incest, or abuse by family members, is committed by a loved one. Then the child reasons, "If Daddy loves me, why would he do this unspeakable thing that makes me feel sad and ashamed?" The only logical sequence to this kind of reasoning is Marie's conclusion—that she herself, in some inexplicable way, was to blame for an occurrence that shamed and sickened her. "I didn't understand what was wrong," Marie says, "but I knew there must be something about me that brought out the worst in my father and made my mother turn away as if she despised me."

Victims of abuse often blame themselves, a response that is encouraged by the parents' projection of blame onto the child, who has no way of defending herself. In addition, psychologists Gail Wyatt and Michael Newcomb point out that the love and attention the young

girl receives during the sexual encounter may be the only loving relationship she believes she deserves.

The metaphor of the red flowers is a symbol of the crushed innocence of the sexually violated child in my poem, "Red Flowers."

The man comes in dark slacks,
dark shirt, leather belt
encircling his waist,
calls to her tenderly
from the darkened passage,
with muscled arms, teeth,
fingers, black boll of himself
crushes the red flower

watches it tear, bleed
though pressed sheets
staining his daughter's
furry rug shaped like
a baby bird.
Blossoms bleed through
tall ceilings, walls
of the house,
dark flowers bloom
from his toothbrush
his comb.

The next morning, waking,
the man doesn't see
giant flowers breaking
from his mouth, his manhood,
crushed blossoms streaming
through aisles of the house.
He shaves, showers
slips into his button-down
shirt crisply starched,
his immaculate blue suit,

drives to his office
where no one sees
the red flower
ripe on his tongue.
The child hides
the torn flower
in a pocket

> behind her ribs
> crowding her heart,
> packs her lunchbox
> walks to school
> a pattern of roses
> etched on her feet.

The "pattern of roses"—the shapes of lost innocence—are etched indelibly on the lives of sexually abused children. And since the abuse for Marie continued into late adolescence and she was powerless to stop it, her negative feelings of disgust and guilt intensified until they became unbearable. It's not surprising that she turned to drugs and alcohol to dull the pain! Research has also shown that abuse ending when the victim is adolescent or in her twenties—as opposed to that ending in childhood—produces longer-lasting more destructive effects on the individual's ability to cope with stress and to form positive relationships with friends or family.

REVERSAL OF THE GENERATIONS AGAIN AND AGAIN

Abused children suffer from feelings of guilt, depression, anxiety, and withdrawal. Such families clearly lack healthy emotional bonds, open communication, problem-solving skills, and defined intergenerational boundaries. They also appear to lack empathy and understanding, possibly because of the sustained denial and repression generated in such an atmosphere.

It seems that the children of abusive families are drafted to meet the parents' needs—and that roles are reversed. Again, as with Amy, Laura, Kate, and Barbara, the "parental child" emerges—the child who must assume an adult role in meeting the parent's need for companionship, counsel, or even sexual gratification.

The saddest part of this unhappy story is that adults who have been abused are more likely to abuse their own children, either emotionally or sexually. The basis for this appalling pattern, although it seems unthinkable, illustrates a basic psychological principle. Since children develop by *modeling* their first personal relationships, abused sons and daughters will expect their children to satisfy adult needs just as they were expected to meet those of their parents. Here we see still another dramatic enactment of *multigenerational transmis-*

sion theory as the chain of pathology is passed on from one generation to the next.

In fact, studies have shown that even when *sexual abuse* is definitely curbed in the multigenerational process, victims of abuse continue to rely on their children to fill their adult *emotional needs*. The task of separating from the parent during adolescence becomes obviously more difficult for the child of a needy mother (or father) since the youngster instinctively responds to the vulnerability of the parent and hesitates to stake out her own claims. And wherever there is great emotional intensity between parent and child, it is almost impossible for the child to declare her independence without feeling overwhelmingly guilty and anxious.

AN ACT OF COURAGE

"When I was fourteen," Marie says softly, "I was in such pain and so confused that I talked to a family friend, someone I felt close to and that I could trust. I couldn't stand it any longer. I confronted my father in front of the whole family and told them all (including the friend) just what had been going on since I was a little girl.

My father denied everything of course, and my brothers and sister were ashamed and scared at the same time. They insisted that I was exaggerating, even making things up because I wanted attention. They knew exactly what was happening, but they couldn't bring themselves to admit that something so horrid could be taking place right in our own house.

My brother, Cliff, at sixteen was feeling so much confusion and anxiety that he had already become a full-fledged alcoholic and cocaine addict. What he didn't want to admit was that during a drunken high, he had molested me too. He just couldn't face that act so he insisted that I was 'betraying the family trust.' Imagine! What trust? I was betraying the dark prison that kept us all locked inside—the shame of sex with your own father—incest! It's even hard for me to say that word now, it's so terrible.

I was amazed at what happened after that. I became the criminal for accusing my father, and he was the victim. My mother blamed me most of all. I could never accept that. How could she love me and allow this to happen to me? But no one would admit to anything, and I was only fourteen so what could I do?"

THE PSYCHOLOGY OF DENIAL

Denial is the psychological defense mechanism used by families wherever there is alcoholism, mental illness, maltreatment, abandonment, or other dark family secrets. Denial is strongest when it comes to the secret that is the most taboo and the most shameful of all—incest. And the response of family member to Marie's confrontation is not surprising when we realize that incest engenders a kind of *cognitive dissonance* that makes it almost impossible for families to recognize sexual abuse. Cognitive dissonance simply means that when our experiences and behaviors differ greatly from our ideas and feelings, we change our perceptions in order to reduce the discomfort we feel.

Barrett and Trepper point out why. A child can't afford to recognize that a beloved parent is exploiting her and causing so much pain. Gradually the child or adolescent may be driven to recognition and confrontation as Marie was in her desperation. But a wife who recognizes the presence of abuse may be forced to leave her husband and faces the prospect of loss of her position in society, loss of any degree of emotional security, and a future of poverty and uncertainty. Siblings may be terrified of the father and of what may happen to them.

It's equally as difficult for the perpetrator of the abuse to come to terms with the harm he is inflicting on his own family. As long as families can deny what is happening—and all members are usually aware of it to some extent—the family can continue to function as a family, get up in the morning, go to a job or school, and attend family and community affairs. But once the truth is out in the open, *change has to occur,* and change is traumatic and painful for both the perpetrator and the family.

Denial on the part of both the abuser and the family goes through a number of stages once it is brought to light. First, there is a *complete denial of facts*—that is, that the abuse ever happened at all. This is the most difficult phase to overcome and may take months for a seasoned professional working with the subsystems of the family to accomplish. However, counseling with all family members can corroborate information and brings out layers of perception that would be impossible to unearth otherwise. And when abuse is acknowledged by several members of the family, the credibility of the offender is undermined in such a way that he may finally begin to admit to reality.

The next stage is often a *denial of awareness.* At this point the abuser admits to the facts but blames the act on being drunk or memory lapses or some sort of traumatic stress. The other parent, the mother, for example, may say that she was asleep or away at the time the molestation took place and didn't know about it. Or she may claim not to remember that her daughter told her what had happened.

When this form of denial is broken, another form often crops up—the offender may propose a *denial of responsibility*. In other words, he suggests that the daughter lured him with seductive speech or dress or asked him a sexual question that he was forced to answer with an explicit demonstration. In many cases the victim herself and/or the mother may take responsibility for the abuse. The daughter may agree that she dressed seductively and the mother will confirm that the daughter is to blame—or she herself, for failing the husband in some way. Or the whole responsibility may be shifted to drugs or alcohol. "He does crazy things when he drinks" or "He's not himself when he's in his cups."

Denial of impact minimizes the severity of the act and the impact of its consequences. Often the offender will say, "It only happened once or twice" or "I never asked her to touch me." He will claim that "it doesn't bother him," "that it happened so long ago it doesn't affect anyone," that "she was just a child and will get over it."

Unhappily, Marie's family has not even begun to face the dark undercurrents of pathology that flow through the family story and can't understand why they constantly feel so much pain and anxiety. Although her brothers and sisters have isolated themselves from their parents, their feelings of shame and self-doubt have never been resolved. Except for Marie, they refuse to recognize the terrible sickness that is poisoning them all.

Denial in all its manifestations has to be overcome if healing is to begin for the offender and his victims. Probably most abusers, even alcoholics and drug addicts, are ashamed of their behavior if they are ever honest with themselves and want the kind of satisfaction that springs out of healthy relationships. But they are certain that if the truth is known, they will be ostracized by relatives, friends, and community. In addition, the offender may face a jail term if he admits to his transgressions. Yet as difficult as it is for the abuser to admit to this dark side of his nature, *it is the only way the circle can be broken*. A man who has molested his own children may molest his grandchildren or his children may abuse their children. Victims and abusers must seek help for the whole family if they are to break destructive patterns in the next generation.

THE LEGACY

"I started drinking at about sixteen, really drinking," Marie continues. "My older brother by then was a confirmed addict, and he went off to a rehabilitation place. He began to look healthier than he had in years and his attitudes started to change. We thought he was going to come out of it okay. Then the heavy drugging started again once he was home. He died at seventeen of a drug overdose.

I didn't know any way to get rid of the awful grief and pain I felt—even though he hadn't always been good to me. I was drinking to keep from feeling anything and was out with my friends all the time, drinking and partying. The boys seemed to like me, and I always had a boyfriend hanging around, not always the best type as you can imagine. Then I started using cocaine, and things went from bad to worse.

I had moved out of our house at least, but the friends who lived with me were big partiers, irresponsible too, didn't pay the bills or take care of the apartment. We were all hooked on something or several things—wine or beer or marijuana or cocaine, you name it. Then they all moved out, leaving me with the rent, utility, and phone bills that had accumulated for several months. It was a nightmare. I'm still paying off those debts.

Finally I lost my driver's license, through a DUI ("driving under the influence"), but I was still functioning enough to keep my job in a health food shop. I loved that job and didn't want to lose that too. I had to move back home in the meantime since I was completely broke. When I finally realized I had to have counseling to pull out of the hole I'd dug for myself, I was desperate. I had no idea of how I'd survive and what to do next. And I still wasn't allowed to lock my door!"

THE OPEN DOOR

Minuchin, known for his pioneering work with adolescent anorexia, relates a case history dubbed the "Open Door" that is famous in the annals of family therapy. The father, a domineering Italian patriarch, would never allow his teenage daughters to lock their bedroom door or even to close it. Although there was no evidence of sexual abuse, Minuchin theorized that the father had taken over every aspect of his daughters' lives. To wrest control back from her father, the fifteen-year-old daughter developed a severe case of anorexia nervosa (the one form of control left to her—her eating habits) and had nearly starved herself to death at the point when the family came to the therapist for help. When the father finally began to recognize the consequences of his behavior, Minuchin insisted that, as part of the therapeutic process, the daughters be allowed to close and lock the bedroom door. Only then could they begin the slow process of recovery. Anorexia is a stubborn illness, and its victims often continue to battle its dangerous recurrences for the rest of their lives.

The trauma of the loss of independence suffered by family members is dramatically symbolized by the metaphor of the "open door" into their lives. Of course the father's invasions of Marie's bedroom were much more than an invasion of privacy—they were brutal violations of her love, trust, and innocence.

A WAY OUT: DRUGS AND ALCOHOL

Children who have been physically abused often demonstrate severe behavioral problems in adolescence—defiance, truancy, vandalism, or open addiction to alcohol and/or drugs. Psychologists Jeffrey Williamson and colleagues theorize that the sexually abused youngster usually keeps her problems to herself and internalizes feelings of worthlessness and guilt. Because of this generalized feeling of shame and low self-esteem, adolescent victims of sexual abuse often don't function well in any areas of their lives. They feel ostracized and emotionally isolated. A sense of disgust and shock at a relationship that is clearly taboo in society yet is supported by the impenetrable family network creates an inner conflict that may well lead to terrible loneliness or even psychotic breakdown.

The breaking of intergenerational boundaries in cases of sexual abuse carries with it a message of ambivalence and shame. The child feels loved only in some terrible, unmentionable way. She loses her sense of identity, and her confusion and anxieties escalate to such an unbearable climax that the only escape she sees is through alcohol and drugs or suicide. The only way to endure the pain is to blot it out. And of course drugs and alcohol do bring some temporary respite, possibly even a feeling of brief happiness, which is soon forfeited when they turn on us and cause a new round of troubles and suffering.

The effects of childhood abuse are complex and long-lasting. Recent research supports the evidence that physical abuse in childhood is a portent of aggressive behavior patterns in later life. A study of physically abused and/or neglected children found that these youngsters are likely to attribute hostile attitudes to others since they grow up feeling that the world is a violent, unpredictable place where every individual must fight desperately and with every resource at her command to survive. Children of abuse may also suffer failures in interpersonal relationships. They develop feelings of abandonment and loneliness—precursors of clinical depression in adulthood.

Loneliness, which has been described by psychoanalyst Otto Will as "the molding force in human relationships," is an inseparable part of the individual make-up and an indisputable part of our intrapsychic experience. However, loneliness takes on a different meaning for the abused or neglected child, who may feel that she is flawed in some irreconcilable way that can never be changed. The family contributes to this myth by selecting this child to become the bearer of the family's unresolved feelings of loss and emptiness or to deflect long-standing problems or conflicts.

Whatever role the child takes on in this family network, she feels lonely because the parent has abdicated the parenting role. We can manage feelings of loneliness if we choose to be alone, but when loneliness and isolation are forced on us, we not only feel alone in the context of the family but alone in the world.

In addition, the child often doubts her own perceptions. Where there is a denial of abuse or addiction (or both), she receives a contradictory message. Although she knows that last night her father was drinking swearing, screaming, and throwing his dinner plate on the kitchen floor, the next day it's as if nothing ever happened. Mom denies the scene, her siblings don't want to talk about it, and no one else seems to be aware of what's going on. As long as denial continues, the family excuses the behavior of the abuser and allows the daughters and sons to grow up with a distorted sense of reality and to believe that it is possible to live in a web of lies and cruelty. Only once denial is broken can healing begin to take place.

HEALING FROM ABUSE

Recovery from sexual abuse is a longtime process. At the same time that the victim feels terrible loss and pain, she also suffers feelings of guilt and shame. Should she feel guilty? Of course not, but we often are not logical beings, and when we have suffered a violation of this magnitude, the scars run deep and long. Any woman who has suffered sexual abuse of any kind is strongly advised to seek counseling.

As part of her recovery, what can Marie do to shore up her boundaries? Now, working closely with a therapist, she has taken several definitive steps by:

1. Moving out of the physical environment of her family home and resolving never to go back.
2. Removing herself from the emotional cycle of bitterness and pain of the parental relationship and admitting to the truth of her experience. Although she feels that she can never forgive either parent for the violations she has suffered, she can begin to forgive herself!
3. Joining with self-help groups such as AA, ACOA and other twelve-step groups not only to help her recover from addiction but also to foster her growth in courage, strength, and self esteem. Within these groups she can find the emotional sustenance, warmth, and feeling of belonging that are missing in her family of origin.
4. Setting limits in her relationships with friends and loved ones. She is learning, slowly and painstakingly, to say no when her rights are threatened or she senses an invasion!

COVERT SEXUAL ABUSE

More subtle forms of sexual abuse often play a hidden part in the drama of family conflicts. Tricia, an attractive redhead in her early fifties, is almost certain her father was sexually attracted to one of her younger sisters. He didn't dare show it openly but concealed his feelings behind a mask of fatherly concern. Tricia tells us,

"Something was going on in my father's head about how he saw my sister Bea as a sex object. To control her he turned her into a 'whore'— he accused her of having sex with everybody and so she did! While still in her teens, she got pregnant and had a baby that she put up for adoption. She did this, I'm sure, to get at my father. It was the perfect revenge, although of course it hurt her more than it did him.

My sister was different from the rest of us. She was very provocative. She attracted animals and brought all the strays home to our house. And she brought the young men home too. Obsessed with the idea of 'looking perfect,' she had a talent for it and she was stunning. The boys started coming round in droves.

At this point my father became involved. He subconsciously wished he could be reaping the benefits of all this sexuality, and of course he couldn't. I remember some strange scene where he was chasing her around outside, but I don't know the particulars or exactly what happened. It had sexual overtones, I know, although I don't think anything actually transpired.

After my father's death, when my mother was in a hospital—trying to overcome the drinking problem that had been her way of dealing with the pain and frustration she felt—Bea wouldn't come out to be part of the family therapy. The hospital wanted all of the family to be involved in the recovery process, but she refused. I think she was afraid of a lot of ambivalent feelings surfacing from that era.

The interesting part of this is that my sister became the caretaker when my father was very ill, just before he died. She seemed to have a need to make up to him for how she had acted in the past toward him. In spite of everything, I believe she always wanted recognition from him. And she wanted him to be a real father."

Hidden or *covert abuse* can be as devastating as active abuse because it's intangible—we can't see it or define it so how can we fight it? Behavior may be orderly, respectful, socially acceptable, but a dark undercurrent of shame and repressed desire runs just below the surface, ready to explode. The adolescent Bea and her sister, Tricia, were well aware that the father's display of parental concern hid barely concealed sexual yearnings. Bea, flaunting her father's will, indulged in promiscuous, self-destructive behavior that would bring chaos into her own life with an unwanted pregnancy. "The perfect revenge," yes, but an act that would cause Bea pain and guilt for a long time to come.

FORGIVENESS: A DEFINITION

Bea's abrupt turnaround at her father's deathbed is not uncommon. Children want to love and respect their parents. They wish desperately to believe in them and trust them. And despite all evidence to the contrary, they continue to hope they will gain recognition and affection from a mother or father incapable of giving it. Our reasoning may be that *if a parent can't love us, then we must not be worthy of love from anyone.* A frightening prospect!

Marie has had to reconcile herself to the fact that her parents are cold, ego-centered human beings, that her father is a violent alcoholic, and that it's okay for her to feel anger at the terrible treatment she received at their hands. She can forgive herself for not loving an

unlovable mother and father. Bea, too, may be coming to the realization that not every individual deserves our love. Although there may
be mitigating factors in a father or mother's background—abuse,
neglect, loss of affection, addiction, poverty, a lack of education—
ultimately every individual is responsible for her own actions.

When we come to the question of forgiveness, we have to ask, if it is
necessary for our own emotional health to forgive those who have
wronged us. No, no, no, we don't! We do have to resolve our feelings
about a parent, to come to terms with unrealistic expectations, and
to begin the long, difficult journey of putting our anger and resentment behind us. But we don't have to forgive an abusive parent. We
have to forgive ourselves.

Why should we have to forgive ourselves when we, the victims, have
done nothing shameful or hurtful? Because we, as abused or neglected
children, have learned our lesson well. We have been taught that we
are to blame for whatever has gone wrong in a parent's life. If it weren't
for us, Mother would be a ballet dancer or a concert pianist; Dad
would be president of a multimillion-dollar corporation; there would
be no financial problems, no arguments, no fights. We have ruined
everything for our parents and must be held accountable. If they didn't
have us to blame, they might have to take a good look at the chaos of
their own lives and actions and how disconcerting, how terrible that
would be.

> . . . Ghosts, I burn them nightly,
> nightly they rise again
> to whimper with the wounded moon,
> each blinded star.
>
> —"A Burning Barrow"

6

Carousel

... But when the music thins,
silver notes slow sliding in,
when the perfect circle ends
where will the children be,
will their hands as smooth as honey,
smooth as water in the cup,
will their hands soon brim to thistle,

will the silken skin yet bloom
to briar and ash and thorn,
and will they, the tan giraffes,
black panthers, smiling tusks,
the painted rabbits wearing white,
will they be crying?

—"Carousel, the Montgomery Mall"

Julia is a lovely, silver-haired woman in her late sixties. Although poised
and well dressed, she speaks in a monotone, her voice barely rising
above a whisper. Her hands tremble, and it seems to be painful for
her to rise from the chair or to answer a simple question.

"It's true—I don't care about anything now," she says quietly. "I
used to love my flowers, especially my roses you'll see out back in
the garden. Now they are dying, consumed with aphids, and turning dry and brittle. Since my husband Allan's death, I try to keep
myself alive, but I never feel like cooking or eating, keeping my
house in order.

I cry easily. In fact, I'm always on the verge of tears. I don't understand why I walk around feeling guilty all the time—as if I were to blame for everything that's gone wrong in the universe. I blame myself for my husband's death. I didn't realize until too late how sick he was because he was something of a hypochondriac. When he really was ill, no one would take him seriously until the very last. Then it was too late. Why didn't I try harder, notice how thin he was, how lethargic? I can't seem to forgive myself."

THE SIGNS OF DEPRESSION

While bouts of the mental illness known as *depression* may strike suddenly and fiercely and then disappear until the next bout, untreated clinical depression may be a long-term, debilitating illness. And it often goes unrecognized because the symptoms appear as physical complaints such as backache, headache, or chronic feelings of fatigue. If a wife tells her husband she is feeling "the blues," he may dismiss her complaint with indifference or even contempt, suggesting that she could easily overcome her lowdown feelings if she "would just stop thinking about herself all the time" or if she "weren't such a crybaby."

Listless and lethargic, she finally drags herself to the doctor—probably her general practitioner who may misdiagnose the symptoms and prescribe vitamins or an exercise regimen. Then she may go to a chiropractor for tense muscles and back pain, to an orthopedist for aching feet, to a minister for family counseling. Again, after countless attempts to find relief, the symptoms of clinical depression will, in all likelihood, go undetected and untreated.

According to a 1992 survey in the *New York Times,* depression has become a major health problem in this country yet has received little public or professional attention thus far. The National Institute of Mental Health reports that depression affects as many as 15 million Americans every year, and that women are twice as likely as men to suffer from this debilitating mental illness.

In fact, the problem has reached such proportions that a national program developed by Harvard University in cooperation with the American Psychiatric Association, Harvard's Department of Psychiatry, and the National Depressive and Manic Depressive Association is now being developed to screen people for depression, alert them to its recognizable signs, and urge sufferers to seek treatment. Early treatment can help reduce the chances of future depression and can shorten the length and the intensity of the illness. Severely depressed people often are suicidal, and in these cases, diagnosis and immediate hospitalization are called for.

What are the symptoms of clinical depression and how do we recognize them? One of the first signs we may notice, particularly in adolescents, are *changes in personality.* The formerly outgoing adolescent becomes moody and withdrawn. She no longer cares if her makeup is sloppy or her blouse is unironed. She is no longer active in the school band or drama group. She *sleeps excessively* and *appears to have no interest* in happenings on the school or social scene. She may even start to *talk of death* and *begin giving away her favored possessions*—an almost certain signal of suicidal thinking.

The symptoms of depression as they emerge in later life are similar, although changes may be more gradual and less noticeable. *Apathy, listlessness, loss of appetite,* and *suicidal ideation* are all marked signs of the onset of depression. For the elderly there is a high correlation between physical illness or disability and depression. *Paranoid thinking* also increases in older people, especially when combined with hearing or sight loss. The elderly often have problems dealing with the losses in their lives and may project them onto the outside world, accusing others of lying, stealing, or cheating.

JULIA'S STORY: APATHY AND DESPAIR

"It's a terrible effort for me to pay my bills," Julia says, clasping her thin hands together tightly. "And I have a constant struggle to keep my house from falling down around me. Yet I don't have the money to pay anyone to do those things for me. I barely get by as it is.

I know I should get out more, see friends, take a walk around the block, but I don't have the will or the energy. Even if my son is coming to visit, I consider it a chore. I have to pull myself out of bed, get dressed, comb my hair. I feel I should get groceries somehow, put a meal of sorts together for the two of us even though he doesn't ask me to. Often I simply can't do it and am still lying in bed when he comes.

And I feel terrible most of the time, maybe because I don't get enough exercise and don't eat what I should. I don't know. I do know my system doesn't work right, and it's an effort for me just to go to the bathroom. I have trouble sleeping too, but when I do finally get to sleep, it takes an earthquake to rouse me.

I used to have friends, but since my husband died, I feel my friends have deserted me. I'm sure that's not true completely—they probably think *I've deserted them.* It's been twelve years since my husband's death, and I still can't seem to pull myself together. I certainly can't sit around drinking coffee and making small talk with people who don't really care about me. Of course, why should they? I'm not much fun to be around.

I feel hopeless. Things look so dark that I've tried to commit suicide twice. The last time I saved up my pills and took an overdose. But my neighbor was concerned when she didn't see any sign of me, and she called my son. They rushed me to the hospital and rescued me. For what reason I don't know. I don't want to continue living if it's going to be like this."

Julia dramatically illustrates many of the common symptoms of depression—feelings of apathy, pessimism, guilt, and loneliness. Depression may also cause memory impairment and a slowdown of all the functions of the brain and body. There is a noticeable loss of appetite and ensuing weight loss, plus insomnia (or excessive sleeping), indigestion, and a host of other physical and emotional disturbances. The depressed individual loses all interest in pleasurable activities, and there is a marked decline in the sex drive.

Depressed people, especially women, are consumed with corrosive feelings of guilt. Anger is often the inverse side of depression, but because such women find it difficult to express anger openly, they experience anger and frustration as sadness, hopelessness, anxiety, and guilt.

Julia feels worthless and useless. She blames herself for all she does or doesn't do—the sins of both omission and commission. "I should work in my garden. . . . I should clean the house. . . . I should cook Easter dinner. . . . I shouldn't burden my children with my troubles." Yet she feels powerless to change her behavior or perceptions. If we look closely, we see patterns of dependency and helplessness emerging throughout her story.

THE PURSUIT OF INTIMACY

"When I was a young woman," Julia says, "I ran my household, took care of my son and daughter. But I never felt confident that I was doing a good job. My husband always felt that family chores were a woman's responsibility and I understood that, yet at the same time I longed for someone who would take care of me. However, my husband worked hard and long hours at his job as a financial consultant so I couldn't expect him to cook and do the dishes or put the children to bed when he came home. I did expect or at least hope for some time together though, some kind of companionship.

But, just like my father, my husband would never let anyone in too close to him and whenever I edged near him, he edged away. He was drinking too much in later years too and started to be suspicious of everyone, including me. I wanted so much to be close to someone that I think I relied too much on my children to give me affection and even to help me make decisions. I've never felt confident about my own choices.

Now I'm afraid—afraid of everything. I'm frightened if I open the front door, have to speak to anyone, take a walk around the block. I can't drive a car anymore. I do when it's absolutely necessary, but I shouldn't because when I drive to the market about a mile away, I sit at the wheel shaking with fear. I tried driving to some self-help meetings that my psychiatrist recommended, but I couldn't make it. I would panic at every light, every turn in the road, afraid of being lost or having an accident. I even tried just going to a friend's house, someone I knew well once, and she was going to take me to my meetings. But I couldn't do it."

THE SEEDS ARE PLANTED EARLY

Research indicates that the cause of depression may sometimes be a genetic legacy although the way in which depression is inherited is unclear and may vary from one family to another. In whatever mode the gene factor plays into the picture, scientists feel that severe depression is probably a result of a lack of chemical neurotransmitters in certain areas of the brain. Often the illness can be successfully treated with medication under the careful supervision of a psychiatrist or qualified physician. But for Julia medication prescribed by her psychiatrist didn't work to relieve her suffering—possibly because of the interworkings of some very complex psychological factors. Julia tells us,

"My mother died when I was only four or five. I didn't have any warning that she was even sick, and I still don't know what happened. No one ever explained it to me or tried to console me, as I remember. I had an older brother, but he was too absorbed in his own grief to take care of a little sister.

Then my father remarried only about a year-and-a-half after my mother's death. Again, no one told me anything. As was probably usual for that generation, my father didn't feel he had to talk to me about his decision, and he thought it would be wonderful for me to have a new stepmother and two stepbrothers and a stepsister. But I never felt loved by my stepfamily. They were so attached to each other, and I never believed I belonged. My stepmother was demonstrative with her own children, but she was strict with me and never loving. My father didn't seem to notice the difference. I grew up feeling lonely and unattractive, and I didn't understand what was wrong with me. However, because I was shy and quiet no one ever knew how miserable I was.

As an adolescent I think I must have been attractive, as the boys were always calling me, and I could project a self-confidence I didn't feel. But my sense of being strange and different didn't go away."

THE SEARCH FOR AFFIRMATION

It seems clear that the need for love and support is not only a requisite for healthy ego development during infancy but also extends well into early childhood and adolescence. In fact, the developing personality continues to need strong affirmation and support *throughout the life cycle* according to Erikson's psychosocial theory.

Erikson believes that a crucial stage of development—*industry versus inferiority*—begins at around age five-and-a-half. At this point the child is building new skills and abilities and is beginning to take initiative in new activities. She may attempt to go to a nearby neighbor's house on her own, or try to find out how a toy works, or what makes a clock tick. This is also an aggressive phase, and she may throw things or kick or hit when things don't work out according to plan.

Erikson suggests that at this point the parent should encourage the child to take the initiative when it's feasible but to place definite limitations on risky ventures. If the child is forceful, the parent may be overly punitive, producing feelings of guilt and resentment, but if parents are too permissive, the child may feel they don't love her because there are no rules to govern her conduct and keep her safe. However, at this stage, if the child does not build skills and competency and learn to take reasonable risks, especially when competing with her peers, she may develop a sense of failure that persists throughout her life.

At this crucial stage in her life, Julia found little support for venturing into new initiatives or little encouragement that she might succeed. But because her father was demanding and often critical, she attempted to please him in spite of the fears that overwhelmed her at every new undertaking. Her stepmother, it seems, was never able to respond with the warmth and reassurance the five-year-old so desperately needed.

When a parent dies, a young child not only suffers a sense of overwhelming loss and isolation, but may even feel she is to blame for the mother's death! Since children have no realistic concept of death, they may believe that an angry remark or even a hostile thought has the power to kill. Julia doesn't recall feeling guilt for her mother's death, but she is certain that her father never gave her the kind of affection she needed at a critical time.

A PRECARIOUS CHILDHOOD

In an unstable world where her chief figure of security—her mother—suddenly died when she was young and vulnerable, Julia suffered very early a loss of security. Major crises in our lives are painful and difficult to cope with under the best of circumstances, and we experience feelings of denial, depression, and anger. Sometimes we repress an experience that is too painful to bear. But children have developed few coping mechanisms, and in a family like Julia's where there appears to be little closeness or communication, the child is left with a sense of confusion, sorrow, and depression. Julia's father, according to her story, was a distant figure with little idea of how to face the strains of his motherless household or to give his children the kind of understanding they needed to withstand this blow at the family core.

His remarriage may have been a natural solace for the father, but it created a threat to Julia—*an invasion of her rights and role as an integral part of the family.* When decisions are made that affect us, even as children, we need to feel that we have some part in that choice. And Julia soon would find herself on the outside looking in—with the intrusion into the family circle of a stepmother, stepbrothers, and stepsisters, all rivals for her father's affections. And they were all, as she perceived it, bonded in a coalition against her. Sadly, Julia's life would be marked from adolescence on by periods of deep depression.

BATTLING THE ILLNESS

Although Julia has never healed from her early traumatic experiences and feelings of loss and estrangement, there are definite steps sufferers can take to define the illness and find relief. What can we learn from Julia's story?

1. Know the signs of the illness—apathy, loss of appetite, lethargy, negative perceptions, thoughts of suicide, and other symptoms.
2. Recognize depression as an illness, not a weakness. Mental illness is still viewed with suspicion and hostility by many in our society. But clinical depression is as serious an illness as diabetes or high blood pressure and should be treated accordingly.
3. Don't blame yourself for a parent's neglect or abuse—you are not to blame for a parent's shortcomings, whatever they are. Actually, blaming ourselves or blaming others for our problems can stunt our emotional growth and the search for constructive solutions.
4. Begin treatment early with a professional therapist. With proper medication and counseling at the onset of depression, the illness can often be relieved in a relatively short time—sometimes a matter of weeks.

THE SEARCH FOR INTIMACY— AND THE LOSS OF SELF

In a groundbreaking analysis of the nature of depression in women, appropriately entitled *Silencing the Self,* Dana Crowley Jack conducted a longitudinal study of twelve clinically depressed women and came up with some intriguing discoveries. In exploring the link between attachment behaviors and depression, Jack found that for many of the women *intimacy was confused with the metaphor of "oneness."* In other words, these women felt that in order to attain true intimacy, it was necessary to merge with the husband or lover, transcending all boundaries and integrating into a whole large enough to contain two separate selves.

Such a concept of intimacy is often fostered by a parent's demand for conformity as a prerequisite for being loved. When these women spoke of merging the personality, they thought in terms of taking on the husband's interests, values, and goals. Since independence of thought is often condemned by the family or society in general, the woman begins to identify any autonomy—voicing her opinions, pursuing her own interests, making her own judgments—as an obstacle to intimacy.

Such an ideal does not suggest that the feminine psyche is basically flawed but simply that women are hearing and responding to the dictates of the culture they have grown up in. Yet the more they strive to attain this impossible ideal, the more they find it necessary to suppress the separate self. And of course the merge of two personalities is always an unequal one, with the woman playing the distinctly subordinate role.

The woman is then asked to suppress the real "I," the core of the self, to gain the respect of her husband and of society. Her healthy need for close, sharing relationships is seen as a feminine weakness instead of a valid desire to build strong, healthy ties.

Such an invasion can occur on a subtle level in a bid for power in the marital or lovers' relationship, but women like this with a flawed sense of identity are, as one psychologist expresses it, "sitting ducks" for major boundary invasions. They are often attracted to men who appear to be strong, the macho, chauvinistic male who actually is insecure and covers up his own feelings of powerlessness with a show of bullying and abuse. These macho males are usually also quite possessive and jealous, which may lead to physical violence or at least emotional abuse. And with the destructive forces of abuse unleashed, the cycle lengthens and becomes more intense. To these depressed women, however, the idea of change is so threatening that they choose to stay in miserable, even dangerous situations rather than risk the challenge of something different.

The connection between boundaries and depression is a highly charged one, it seems. When our boundaries begin to dissolve, when we suppress the inner voice, when our goal in a relationship is to please the other person no matter how much anxiety, anger, and frustration we may feel, then the sense of self diminishes, becoming smaller and smaller, until it is almost extinguished.

DEPRESSION AND THE LOSS OF SELF: PEGGY'S STORY

It's been ten years since Peggy, a tall, gregarious redhead, divorced her husband Richard. A physical education teacher in the local high school and an accomplished athlete, Peggy, the attractive, self-contained person we see today, had become a listless, frightened figure by the time her marriage ended.

"When Richard left," Peggy relates, "he took everything with him—my energy, my vitality, my love of tennis, golf, swimming, my faith, my confidence, everything. I was just a ghost, and not even a very healthy ghost. I had to drag myself to my job every day. It was a chore for me to get out of bed, to speak, to eat, to laugh. I didn't laugh much, I can tell you. There wasn't much to laugh about. He had abandoned me in every sense of the word, left me with a leaking roof, a car in need of repairs, two hurt, rebellious teenagers, no money, and no idea of how I was going to pay the bills.

In fact, we had never talked about money. Early in our marriage, in fact, from the very beginning, he handled the bills. That was fine with me then as, fresh out of college, I didn't know the first thing about finances. My father had always handled everything, given me money, paid the bills. Even after I started working my junior year in college, I pretty much turned my finances over to my father. I paid for my personal expenses and entertainment, but he took charge of everything else. Even now my father doesn't think I can balance my checkbook!

At the beginning of our marriage Richard was starting his MBA program and I taught school. The money I earned then I gave to him without question to pay for our expenses. After our son was born, I still worked part-time as a substitute and my parents helped us out financially. Then again when we bought our first house, his parents gave us the downpayment, and my parents gave us the carpeting, the appliances, and whatever else we needed. Looking back on it, I now realize that neither one of us was very smart about money—we were always dependent on somebody else to keep up our lifestyle. Not that he wasn't a hard worker; he was super intelligent and worked long hours for a big corporation in the city, but it was never quite enough. He had high aspirations, and I just followed him blindly.

He never indicated in any way that we were overspending or that he was stressed out about money or anything else. He was incredibly private, and if I tried to find out our economic status, he would either ignore me totally or yell at me. I should have taken his extreme reactions as a warning signal that something was wrong, but I steered away instead. I was afraid to look at what might be happening.

We experienced some rough spots in our life together for a while, but basically I felt we had a good marriage. He was wiry and strong, not really handsome, but so ambitious and gifted that I thought I was lucky to be married to such a paragon. He seemed to adore our two children, would do anything for them, but at the same time he was strict with them, demanding that they take on responsibilities and keep up their grades in school. He did a lot of work around the house too. He could fix anything and whatever he did, it was perfect.

Richard was intensely competitive although it didn't always show on the outside. But he couldn't stand for me to beat him at a game of tennis or even a friendly bowling match. And yet we both loved sports and the kind of exhilaration you get from excelling at tennis or golf, the feeling that you are a highly-tuned instrument with your whole body working at capacity. But the difference was that I didn't feel I had to prove myself to anyone else. If I lost, maybe it was a little disappointing, but I preferred to play a close game that was exciting and a challenge; for him it was all in the victory. He seemed to need a lot of reassurance that he was talented, skilled, a winner—which he was or would have been if his attitude hadn't spoiled everything for him and for me.

You have to understand that Richard's father was an authoritarian person, very domineering and cold. He had three boys and a daughter who could never please him, no matter how hard they tried. Richard, for instance, was an honors graduate of his prep school and graduated at the top of his MBA class at the university. Still his father never demonstrated that he was proud of him or that his accomplishments were special. The father was a miserable person, I think, very critical, unlike Richard's mother, a mild, reserved woman who seldom spoke out and was almost a recluse. I'm sure feelings were seldom expressed in that household, and if they ever were, his father would have shot them down immediately.

As a result, Richard didn't want to talk about what was driving him or to ever admit any weakness; so to live with him I had to suppress my natural feelings. And as I'm a pretty open person, it was difficult for me to just shove all I was feeling into the bottom drawer and forget about it. I thought *I* must be doing something wrong because he was so unhappy most of the time. I reached the point where I blamed myself for all of our problems although somehow I knew this wasn't the whole picture. I tried desperately to talk things out with him. I was hoping that my husband, whom I had always considered to be my best friend, could reveal himself to me because he knew how much I loved and admired him."

In the poem "Keeping Silent" the woman seals herself off from all communication because she fears total disintegration if she hears, speaks, does anything to break the silence. And if her life should fall to pieces at her feet, there is no one she can trust to put it back together again. But when we silence the self, we also run the risk of ego disintegration, a suppression of the personality that leads to shame, isolation, and eventually deep despair.

> She could hear everything
> and speak if she wanted to.
> But if she did she thought
> it would be as though
> something breakable
> were carried to the roof
> and dropped off.
> And even if the experts
> gathered it up
> and put it back together
> and even if the people
> who lived with her felt,
> disregarding the cracks,
> that it was as good as new,
> she wouldn't take the chance
> she couldn't trust the glue.

> —by Nancy Ornstein

RIGID BOUNDARY LINES

Although Peggy actively denied the mounting problems in her marital relationship, we sense a number of factors that made the dissolution of her marriage almost inevitable. First, there was little, if any, communication, between husband and wife. Richard, having been brought up in a demanding, perfectionist household, expected perfection of himself, and to communicate feelings of insecurity or vulnerability would have meant that others saw him as less than perfect. In Richard's family of origin there were *rigid individual boundary lines* and little expression of affection or support, and Richard would carry these patterns into his marriage as well as unresolved problems of insecurity and dependency.

In Richard's family appearances—clothes, manners, perfect grooming—counted for everything. Even if a pervasive cancer spread under the skin, no hint of sickness could ever be given to the outside world. Although a great deal was expected, there was little recognition from Richard's parents of even the highest accomplishments. His father, a cold, domineering person, never gave his sons and daughter a strong enough sense of self that they could cope with being vulnerable. If they failed, it was a devastating loss, but no one was there to back them up whether they won or lost.

Richard may have been attracted to Peggy in the first place because of the warmth and openness of her big Irish family. Yet he found it impossible to break out of the thick shell that enclosed him. The "sins of the fathers" are surely visited upon the generations unless we find a way to break the pathological chain, and Richard followed the pattern that had been set for him early in his life. *Never, never say what you feel or the shell may crack, leaving nothing but emptiness. Nothing but shadows.*

Peggy, in trying to please her adored husband, found it necessary to suppress her natural honesty and openness. There were many things she couldn't talk about, and if she did attempt to "strip away" her husband's facade, she discovered a deep anger she couldn't contend with. She couldn't ask if there was anything she could do to help him financially because she had no idea what their financial status was. She was holding down two part-time jobs, but neither of them paid very much, and maybe they couldn't afford the move they had made into a more expensive home. Although she suspected that their lifestyle was overly extravagant and knew that Richard had borrowed money from his father once or twice to finance these undertakings, she couldn't be sure since he refused to communicate with her. Because of his own insecurities, he could never treat her as a partner whose judgment and common sense he respected. He was the patriarch, making all the decisions, while he actually longed for someone to take care of him! In the meantime, the bills were piling up, Richard's anxiety was building to an explosive level, and he was trapped inside his carefully constructed prison. But beneath the surface feelings of rage and self-doubt stirred, ready to erupt at times of stress. A major eruption was already on its way and Peggy and the two children would be caught in the deluge.

SCENES FROM A MARRIAGE: THE DISSOLUTION

"About six years before he left for good," Peggy relates, "Richard became restless and tense. When I tried to talk with him, find out what was bothering him, he would become angry. We were beginning to grow far apart. He had never cared about having a drink before, just an occasional glass of wine, but he began to drink a great deal and come home later each evening, often not until the early hours of the morning. He kept me almost completely out of his life and wouldn't even call to tell me that he would be coming home late. I was tense and nervous too, but I tried to deny that anything was seriously wrong. I kept telling myself it was 'just a phase.'

This pattern continued for the next several years until one evening he came home to tell me he had made an appointment with a marriage counselor for us. During the counseling session Richard announced calmly that he didn't think he loved me anymore. I was stunned, but the therapist was reassuring and just said we had a lot of work to do. I didn't know then that this would be our first and last counseling session.

About a month later I was just getting the kids to bed when he charged into the house and announced he was leaving. He refused to tell me where he was going. He left me with very little money, and I was naturally distressed. So were the children, but with the help of my parents and our priest we pulled ourselves together. Richard would call a few nights each week to talk with us and tell us where he could be reached.

Gradually he began to come home on weekends and then during the week. We only talked on a superficial basis. He said he didn't want to discuss what had happened and would never 'bare himself.' I had never asked him to but would have liked to have some hint of what was going on with him. A few weeks later he came by, apologizing for causing me and the children such pain, and said this would never happen again.

Ten months later he finally did come back. For the next few years our daughter, who was just ten years old, would wake up in the middle of the night asking if her father was home. Our son was seven and we never talked about how his father's absence affected him, but it did a great deal, I'm sure. It had to."

DEFENSE MECHANISMS: WE DENY REALITY

Because Peggy had so tightly suppressed her own very real frustration over Richard's refusal to communicate with her, she tried to stem her anxiety with denial, rationalization, and comparisons: *denying* that there were painful issues that had never been resolved; *rationalizing* that Richard was going through a difficult phase and would soon snap out of it; *comparing* her marriage to others where problems were more openly expressed and seemed, on the surface, more insurmountable. The elephant stepped on her toes more than once, and she never even said "ouch." She never admitted that when the elephant steps on your toes, it hurts!

"Since Richard was such a closed person, I never found out why he left or even why he came back," Peggy relates. "But for the next several years we continued to live together as husband and wife and we had few arguments—except when it came to money. Whenever I started to ask questions about our financial situation or if I tried to delve too deeply into what our relationship had become, he would go into a rage, screaming that he had no time to discuss the situation or totally ignoring me. I decided it was better to stay away from such volatile topics.

On the surface things seemed to be going well for us, and at this point he suggested that I take a political science course at the local adult school with him. Government and politics had never been my strong suit, but I was thrilled that he wanted to include me. After finishing a few classes, we gradually dropped it and never discussed it again."

A MARRIAGE OF SHADOWS

"Then I began to have these terrible anxiety attacks. My heart would begin beating very fast and I couldn't catch my breath. I think now I was submerging all my anxiety about the marriage, and this is how it came out. But I didn't tell anyone what was bothering me because I was afraid to. Once I did drive myself to the hospital emergency room, but they couldn't find anything physically wrong, and the interns probably thought I was just another hypochondriac.

Both of our children began to have problems too. My son started to stutter whenever he was excited or upset and was acting up in school, and my daughter was sick a lot of the time—sore throats, flu, bronchitis, everything. Richard began yelling about medical bills, and I was depressed and angry. I simply couldn't believe how unsympathetic he was toward the daughter and son he had loved so much.

Not long after that the walls came tumbling down. Richard was working on office papers and I was reading the newspaper when he suddenly looked up and said very calmly, 'I'm moving out.' He gathered up his clothes and a few things and moved into an apartment. I just stood and watched him, trying not to show how upset I was—playing the part of the dutiful wife even when my marriage had fallen into pieces at my feet.

Now I realize our marriage was all shadows, nothing but shadows. When I tried to hold onto it, there was nothing there. Richard was a shadow too—he couldn't be a real flesh and blood person because he never dared reveal what he was feeling. It was too dangerous for him because what he was feeling, I suspect, was a lot of anger. Anger at his father, at circumstances, at our financial situation, which I found to be pretty shaky after he left. He couldn't face up to not being a perfect person, that he was vulnerable too.

I think I was devastated because it was the death of an idyll, a dream I had carefully built up for the twenty years of our marriage. I had thought (although not consciously of course) that if I didn't look at our problems, maybe they would disappear. What disappeared was our marriage and Richard. I mourned the death of the dream for a long time. I was a shadow, too, back then. I looked like an actual woman, but there was nothing there.

I was so depressed I could barely get out of bed mornings and I couldn't eat at all. I didn't want to see anyone but my closest friends because I was so stricken. And I couldn't keep my terrible secret hidden any longer. All that mattered to me was my lost marriage, and what kept me going at all was the necessity to provide for myself and the kids and the hope that Richard would change his mind and we could work things out. In the midst of all his cruelty to me, the angry phone calls, his indifferent treatment of our two wonderful children, I wanted him back. Now, looking back on it, I can't believe I ever did. What would I do with him? You can't talk with a shadow or hold him in your arms."

IS INTIMACY A THREAT?

For Richard any step that Peggy took toward establishing a closer relationship became a very real (if unconscious) threat. From his cold, authoritarian father he had learned how to protect himself, how to survive—*don't ever reveal your weaknesses to anyone or you won't be loved.* In order to preserve his armor, Richard's energy went into maintaining what Carl Jung identifies as the *persona*, the face we show to the outside world. His suits were elegant and beautifully tailored, he lived in a lovely house, his manners were polished and polite. He had identified so closely with the outer facade that, as Jung cautions us, there was danger of losing touch with the inner psyche, the real "I." Beneath this seemingly placid surface stirred a sea of volcanic emotions, ready to erupt.

Peggy's depression after the breakup of her marriage stemmed not only from a sharp sense of loss but also from the gradual deterioration of ego and self-esteem in an attempt to close off her real feelings. Like the severely depressed women who participated in Jack's study, she began to feel that her legitimate needs for closeness and trust in a relationship were negative and dependent—not a true desire for healthy intimacy—and that she was not entitled to express them. And, in another striking parallel to Jack's subjects, she had entered into the marital relationship as a strong, stable personality but as she began to view the attachment through Richard's skewed perceptions, she devalued herself accordingly.

Most of us honestly feel we want intimacy in our closest relationships. But real intimacy implies risk. It means that we open ourselves to another person, that we confess our secrets, our dreams, our hopes, our weaknesses. We become vulnerable! And intimacy, as opposed to distance, may engender greater conflict—or at least greater open conflict—because feelings are expressed directly and honestly. To attain intimacy in any relationship we need a sure sense of self, the feeling that we can make choices without fear of blame or anger. We also need defined boundaries that give us a clear map of where to draw the line between the warmth, communication, and sharing that characterize intimate relationships and invasive relationships that are predicated on control and dependency.

PEGGY'S LESSONS

What can Peggy's story teach us? Peggy has learned the difficult lessons of recovery slowly and painfully, but in order to heal from the losses of the shattered ego, the bitterness of separation and divorce, she resolves to:

1. Live in the present. When we live in the past, we constantly submerge ourselves in the grief and suffering of our past lives, lives we can't change no matter how much we want to. And when we live in the

future, we live in a fantasy world that never allows us to take pleasure in today.

2. Set limits in relationships. When Richard erupted with anger, even rage, at her attempts to discover the source of their conflicts, Peggy was frightened and backed away from any confrontation instead of attempting to resolve the real issues between them. She might have stated that although she loved Richard and wanted to help him, she could no longer tolerate the blame and insults heaped on her as the target of his anxiety and frustrations. Once she established clear boundaries, then she could define the consequences of his behavior whenever he stepped over distinctly delineated boundary lines. (When such volatile issues are discussed in a charged emotional atmosphere, the presence and counsel of a therapist are highly recommended.)

3. Let go of attempts to control. What we try to control ends up controlling us! Peggy's feelings that she could somehow have controlled Richard's behavior forced her to live in a state of confusion and anxiety—until she had to admit she could no longer control either circumstances or the dissolution of her marriage.

4. Let go of denial. Sometimes we need the protective mechanism of denial (as Peggy did) to keep us from feeling too much shock and pain, but in order to move on and to heal from traumatic experiences, we have to stay in touch with our feelings and look clearly at the reality of our lives.

5. Build a strong sense of identity through her accomplishments. In Peggy's case, her caring relationships with her students and her own two children and her success as a teacher and mentor have given her the necessary strong sense of self.

There were doors
you missed somehow
lost in the fog or caught
behind a shadow, traces

of a pattern falling into place,
heavy cathedral portals, gaudy
paintings of the saints, a twisted
Christ, rose burnished windows.

In another time
a carved door opened,
a polished knob, smooth, almost
golden, a jeweled eye beckoning.

The hollow frame of brass
burned white ashes in your path

that door closed so softly,
softly latched behind you.

—"The Loneliness of Doors"

7

The Dark Angel

A hand touches your bed
and down the street
a car skids into a giant oak.
This is not your child
lying in the white hospital
with a broken spine, closed lungs,
not this time
but the dark angel hovers
singing prophecies,
a prowler waits
at the midnight door
your daughter opens
your son falls asleep,
a live cigarette falls from loosed fingers,
imagination shrieks and howls
as the dark angel
flies into the distance
busying himself with floods, fires,
other calamities,
climbs a blue-bleached sky
filled with clouds,
sits at the flowery edge,
a random spit of Paradise,
the black ice cracks, wicks flicker,
lighted candles choke and die,
from time to time
the sigh of invisible wings
touches your arms,
your eyelids flutter,

startled, you wake wondering why
your thin dreams tremble.

—"The Dark Angel"

"I was never allowed to express my feelings or ideas. Mostly, I didn't try to. The family structure revolved around Mother's needs and moods. Early, just a little girl still, I became my mother's counselor."

These are Sophia's words. And hers is the story of a child, a brilliant, gifted musician, forced into a symbiotic relationship with her mother, a depressive, needy woman who appropriated her daughter's life as her own.

A SYMBIOTIC LIFE

Sophia's sensitive oval face is shadowed, and her dark eyes grow darker as she relates:

"My mother's parents never gave her anything. My grandmother was manipulative and cold and she played her three daughters against each other so they didn't even have each other to fall back on. She didn't like physical contact of any kind. My grandfather was an absolute maniac, throwing things and screaming whenever he felt like it. No, he wasn't a drinker but definitely a severe paranoid. They were not 'nice people.'

I think he (my grandfather) suffered from a real personality disorder. He couldn't stand touching, even the sight of it. He was naturally very uptight about sex. Physical contact really put him off. He was always shouting to 'leave him alone.' He and my grandmother were quite a pair.

As a consequence, my mother was strange. She could be affectionate if her own needs were being met. She wanted to have a real bond between us, but it had to be on her terms. I did almost all the giving. If I ever tried to express a feeling of disappointment or anger, she would negate it immediately. 'How could you feel that way . . . of course Mrs. B. likes you . . . that's just your imagination.' It was hopeless to try to express myself. Then if I ever did get my disappointment or anger across, I would feel guilty because I'd made my mother feel worse.

My parents discovered early that I was musically gifted. Mother had a symbiotic thing with me—I was supposed to fulfill all her hopes and expectations. I played the piano, starting about age four, and she had always wanted to be an artist. She had terrible feelings of despair and hopelessness, and my role was to make her feel better by filling it with exciting things.

Mother was definitely a talented artist. She made wonderful drawings, but her parents didn't give a damn. Part of my understanding of her comes from knowing her parents. They were not interested in anything aesthetic or creative. Mother was offered scholarships to schools and colleges, but she never took advantage of them. She wouldn't pursue any of her ambitions, probably because she didn't have the confidence.

I was Mother's caretaker. My father was loving and kind, but he didn't want to be responsible for my mother's state of mind so he would say things like 'Why don't you go talk to Mommy . . . she's feeling depressed.' And he would rush into the kitchen to read his newspaper. I was the safety valve. I stayed home. I practiced piano, and I did my homework. I had no childhood.

When I was about four-and-a-half, the real 'meshuga' began—that's the Yiddish term for craziness. My mother was getting worse and worse, and no one knew what to do about her terrible spells of depression and her wild demands.

Then and in grammar school I had few friends. I would be relieved to see my father's parents sitting on the porch when I came home from school so I wouldn't have to deal with my mother. Some of my sanity came from them and from my friends and teachers who took an interest in me."

THE DISSOLUTION OF BOUNDARY LINES

We clearly see, as Sophia's story unfolds, the distortions of the symbiotic relationship between mother and child—a mother who lived through her daughter's experiences, who used threats of her fragile mental and physical health to keep her children and husband in line, demanding their time, energy, and companionship. The expectations of the unfulfilled parent were transferred into the lifeblood of the daughter. The daughter's life, both figuratively and literally, became her mother's. In Sophia's case, since she was precocious and a creative, sensitive person, her burden was doubled. She not only had to fill the emotional void her mother felt, but she had to become the artist her mother never dared to be.

How did Sophia's mother grow into a dependent, depressive woman with little or no respect for her children's feelings or ambitions? Sophia looks at her grandparents and understands that her mother became a neurotic, needy person because she had been denied any nurturance or affection from her own parents. And according to the Mahler's theories, nurturance and close bonding with the mother or caregiver is necessary if the infant is to successfully separate from mother in the separation-individuation phase, which begins at around six months. If the child develops a sure sense of her own worth with an early bond to the maternal figure, then she will develop a cohesive sense of self, an ability to delay gratification, tolerate frustration, and achieve competency.

What chance did Sophia's mother ever have of developing into an independent functioning person? Her mother was manipulative and distant, her father a moody man, maniacal in his outbursts and violent mood swings. Neither parent (Sophia's grandparents) could stand physical contact, even with their own grandchildren or great-grandchildren. "My grandfather couldn't even stand to see me embrace my own son," Sophia says. "That's how bizarre he was." Sophia's mother grew up with strong feelings of loss and abandonment that she couldn't overcome in the course of a long lifetime.

GENERATIONAL ROLE REVERSAL

"I was never a child," Sophia continues. "I always associated with adults so I understood them better. I felt different from all the other kids when I was in grammar school, partly because of my background and partly because I was artistically inclined. And I always had to rush home to take care of my mother or to practice piano. The other kids didn't relate. They would make fun of me for having to stop in the middle of a game and run home.

Then when I went to the Fine Arts High School, things changed. I had more in common with the other students, and I had a few friends. But I don't remember bringing friends home. I don't think my sister or I ever did. My mother was a fastidious housekeeper and a fingerprint on the wall was a major crime. And children, even teenagers, were noisy, never still.

It definitely was not okay for me to fail at anything, or even to accomplish less than my parents felt I was capable of. My mother would have one of her tantrums if there was any hint I wasn't doing the very best. I couldn't even sit still to draw or play with clay; there was never any space for me to enjoy myself. To an extent, because of that early training, I've never learned to relax, just 'veg out and sniff the roses.' Life was pretty grim and there was no joy in it.

Mother's link to me was murky. Very ambivalent. There was a lot of love but also a lot of cruelty. If I didn't feel like practicing, she would threaten to cut off my lessons. And she wasn't even paying for them because I won grants and scholarships that took care of them, but I didn't know that as a child. I knew she was in charge! She didn't hesitate to use any means to get me to do what she wanted. I believe that in her destructive way she really loved me, but it's very hard to extricate yourself from the stranglehold of that kind of love.

It was not only okay for me to succeed, it was necessary! Mother wasn't jealous because I was her surrogate—there was no dividing line between us as far as she was concerned. Something else that was happening was weird. Whenever I would give a musical performance (and this happened fairly often, as I became a professional performer at age nine or ten), Mother would be so preoccupied with her looks and what she would wear on these occasions that my own needs would be totally overlooked. I was invited to do all sorts of performances and we went to some elegant homes for these soirees. And yet she didn't seem to notice if I had outgrown my dress or my shoes were scuffed. Mother would claim that when they met her, they would think less of *me* unless *she was perfectly groomed*. She was always center stage—*her* appearance, *her* feelings, *her* ego. You can imagine how confusing and frustrating that was for me. I desperately needed reassurance, and I wanted to cry out, 'What about me?' But I never did.

As far as material things went, I could ask for things—although of course I didn't often get them because we barely squeaked by. My father worked for an insurance company and he worked very hard, but those were difficult times. My mother made herself busy to the point of exhaustion, cleaning and re-cleaning. You could literally eat off any floor in her house. That's where all of her energy went since she had no social life and no creative outlets of her own.

When it came to any kind of emotional support, I wasn't going to get that. My mother needed everything the family could give her, and there wasn't much left over for anyone else."

THE UNDIFFERENTIATED RELATIONSHIP

The bond between Sophia and her mother that could have been a real link, the love of music, became for Sophia a kind of slavery. "I had to practice, practice, practice," Sophia tells us. There was no time for playing games with friends, even for the solitary amusements of molding clay, drawing, or tea-time with her dolls.

Sophia began to doubt her own identity. When she wasn't practicing piano or doing homework, she was expected to sit at her mother's side, giving her news or gossip, trying to cheer her out of her terrible depressions, attempting to resolve her unresolvable problems. Sophia's own social life, friendships, her energy were sacrificed to keeping Mother happy. No price was too high to pay because Mother might otherwise sink further into grief and depression, might even commit suicide! And yet Sophia's mother is still alive and kicking at eighty-two!

"I was never a child." Does this plaintive comment from Sophia sound familiar? It might remind you of your role in the family system. The paradigm of turning the family hierarchy upside down happens to so many of us that we begin to think it's the usual way things are— the child is supposed to take care of the parents' needs. We have seen this reversal illustrated in the lives of Laura, Amy, Ellen, and Kate but never more dramatically than in Sophia's history where her entire childhood was devoted to saving Mother!

Generational role reversal is definitely a *boundary invasion*. A child is asked to sacrifice her pursuits, energy, and time to take care of Mother or Father. When a mother abandons her role of adult responsibility and her identity as a parent, the daughter loses any idea of who she is or of how to set limits. Is she child or woman, student or teacher, daughter or mother, friend or caretaker? She has no way of knowing because the family hierarchy has dissolved and the intergenerational roles are inextricably mixed.

Sophia and her mother illustrate a classic example of *weak individual boundaries* or *fusion*. The mother desperately yearned for success and recognition, not for herself but for Sophia because there was no "dividing line" between them. Sophia's portrait of Mother clearly illustrates Bowen's portrait of the *undifferentiated* or *fused person,* who has no clear self-image and whose responses are determined almost entirely by emotion. To strive for success on her own would have constituted a real threat to Mother because there was risk involved. She might try and fail! If Sophia failed to live up to expectations, then Mother could still withdraw her support and blame her daughter for the consequences.

Even in high school, as Sophia began to live a less constricted life and find a congenial milieu with students who were, like her, artistic, creative, and "different" from anyone else, she was bound by the invisible wires so skillfully manipulated by Mother. She felt sad and guilty when she spent time with her friends or even indulged in solitary pursuits that were fun, funny, or frivolous.

RIGID FAMILY BOUNDARIES:
THE FAMILY ISOLATES ITSELF

"My parents tried to totally control my thoughts. The family belief system was rigid. Nothing came in. Nothing went out. They could never comprehend if you liked someone they disapproved of or if you liked a different kind of music, anything other than classical actually. I remember a really ridiculous incident when my mother asked my son, 'How can you like listening to that awful jazz? It's just a lot of noise if you ask me.' And his father, my husband, is a professional jazz musician!

That shows you how completely circumscribed she is. Anything new, strange, foreign was anathema to my parents. My father adapted to my mother's modes—they danced the same ballet, which I think happens to some extent to any couple who stays together for a long time. He had to protect himself against her moods, her depression, her demands. She could make life miserable for him—and did.

My mother was smart and artistic too, but she didn't have the emotional balance to use her intelligence and talents. When I was a teenager she went through another series of breakdowns. It was hellish, really hellish. She became severely paranoid, and no psychologist or therapist could help her. She would get the idea that the therapist didn't like her or he wore a wrinkled suit or smoked—any rationalization would do. She couldn't attach to any of them because *they might ask her to change. I* was her counselor. She knew she was safe with me. I would never argue with her or confront her.

My mother told me everything, my father nothing. He believed, and still does, in 'holding your cards close to the chest.' Very German. I have a lot of him in me in that respect. I have friends who tell me I am a closed book, an anachronism in this age of support groups, encounter groups, holding hands, telling all. I can listen to friends, talk to them about ideas, but I don't want to talk about myself, my feelings, what's really going on inside. I think I'm still trying to protect myself against Mother's constant invasions.

My father was distant in the sense that you never knew what he was thinking. He wasn't physically demonstrative either although I knew he loved me. Basically, however, his idea was to do what Mommy says, answer her demands. After a while I would make those demands on myself—anticipating what would keep her happy."

SOPHIA—THE FAMILY HERO

Although boundaries between Sophia and her mother were weak and undefined, the family isolation was kept in place by *rigid family boundary lines between them and the outside world.* With rigid external boundary lines, the invisible walls that define our perimeters are thick and impenetrable. Nothing enters or leaves. In Sophia's family new ideas, new friends, or cultural experiences were rarely, if ever, allowed to penetrate the inflexible borders drawn up to protect the family from change. There was seldom any interchange of ideas with friends and relatives, or getting together with acquaintances inside or outside the extended family circle to celebrate special occasions.

Sophia doesn't recall ever bringing friends home. They might have disrupted the mother's obsessive cleaning, left fingerprints on the wall, or revolutionized the family's ethos with fresh ideas, even a new freedom. And of course the family always had to protect the family "secret," the shameful secret that Mother was childish, temperamental, constantly on the verge of tears or rage.

Sophia, a naturally sensitive sympathetic child, could never rebel against the mother's most outrageous invasions of her needs, her privacy, her life. She was immediately triangulated into the family network as the *savior* or *hero.* In contrast her sister, Baba, became the family *scapegoat,* earning the blame and anger for all the family's hidden conflicts. If Mother was feeling depressed, it was not because of her own frustration and unresolved problems but because Baba was not doing well in school, staying out late, or smoking cigarettes. And Baba rebelled against the parental injunction (unspoken but nevertheless very real) "to take care of Mother." To protect herself against the mother's constant demands, she stayed away from home as much as possible, refused to practice piano although she was musically talented, refused even to go to college because this is what her parents wanted for her!

"My sister is seven years older than I am," Sophia explains. "She resolved her differences with my mother by staying away from home. A lot of people thought I was an only child, and the same held true for my sister—because of the age difference and because she was never home. My sister was busy rebelling against my parents. She didn't want any part of the family scene. Her acting out was probably much healthier than my passive stance.

She married at eighteen, probably to get out of the house. We both married decent men like my father, but my sister has never fulfilled even a small part of her potential. She has 'brains to burn,' but she never went to college because that's what my parents wanted. Instead she got a commercial degree and became a secretary. She could have been a lawyer, in fact, was a legal secretary. She has a wonderful mind and is talented too.

Today I think she is probably a lot less healthy than I am emotionally. Now *she* has the family pathology. Her husband is a difficult guy although they are still together. He doesn't communicate well and has a far-out sense of humor. My sister looks like my mother. I look more like my father, and though my life has been a 'major torment' in some ways, I think I unconsciously identified with the healthier parent. My sister and I have maintained a close relationship in spite of our personality differences and the gap in our ages. We talk to each other everyday."

Sophia, as the family hero, was designated to bring honor to the family name with her gifts and accomplishments, to feed her mother's starved emotional life. In addition, she would be her mother's comforter, entertainer, and protector. In the meantime, her father could retreat behind his shield of reserve and distance himself from his wife's impossible expectations. The unspoken conflicts between husband and wife could be smoothed over, with Sophia and her sister as the focus of the triangle, the objects of all the suppressed feelings. But if Sophia ever stepped out of line by rebelling against her mother's demands, she would be instantly transformed into the *scapegoat*, bearing the brunt of her mother's anger and frustration.

INVASIONS: NO SEPARATE LIFE FOR SOPHIA

"I never had any rights," Sophia says, her voice breaking slightly as she remembers. "My mother always had to be 'inside my head.' She was a compulsive talker, and I was her audience and her entertainment.

She tried to relate her depression and paranoia to symptoms of menopause. But her craziness started a lot sooner. These bouts were all through my adolescence, in fact, my whole childhood. Just as I hadn't been allowed to be a child, I couldn't be a teenager either. I was always forced to be my mother's support, to rush home from wherever I was to take care of her. It never occurred to me to say, 'stop!'

She had no respect for my possessions either. Things would disappear, a sweater, a blouse, a book. She would give them away or throw them out.

I had no rights and no privacy. We moved to a smaller apartment when I was in high school, and I literally had no room of my own. I slept in the living room as there was only one bedroom, my parents'. Physically and emotionally the three of us were right on top of each other. Even when I had a room of my own earlier, no one had ever knocked on the door. They never thought of such a thing.

Mother even read my love letters, letters written by my husband before we were married. She would open my letters before I could! I would never do anything about it, never blew up at her. Can you believe that? I would humor her, cajole her, try to make things right for her because I thought she was 'delicate.' Looking back on it, I remember a phrase from Oscar Wilde—'the tyranny of the weak.' I was afraid she would do something horrible, start ranting and raving, even commit suicide. Now she's over eighty years old and still going strong!"

INVASIONS: THEY NEVER STOP

Growing up, Sophia had *no privacy emotionally.* Her mother was always "inside her head," fastening onto Sophia for sustenance, relentlessly seeking to implant her own visions in her daughter's brain and heart. Nothing strange or alien must be allowed to permeate, and, as we have witnessed in many of these stories, any suggestion of change was a threat—an unconscious threat but nevertheless a very real one that Sophia's mother would meet with every defense she could muster, including denial, projection of guilt, repression, blame, and threats of self-destruction. And, to protect himself and his sanity, her father danced the same steps. The family focus was on Mother, and her needs were overwhelming.

Sophia was never allowed to have any *physical privacy* either. When she was an adolescent, the family moved to smaller quarters—a tiny one-bedroom apartment where Sophia slept on the sofa. She couldn't close or lock her door (not that she had been allowed to previously), but now she literally had no door! Her life, her every activity was exposed to full view. Her mother even read her love letters from her future husband, opening them before Sophia could.

The amazing part to Sophia now is that she never even protested this blatant invasion of the most personal nature! She couldn't bring herself to confront her mother in any way because by this time the implicit message was so deeply engrained—"Mother is fragile." A cross word, an argument could upset her. Or, more dramatically, "Don't rock the boat or Mother may fall into the sea and drown."

The generational division between Sophia and her mother disappeared as Sophia's mother confided in her, telling her intimate, disturbing details about her sexual history, asking for her counsel in matters her daughter was much too young to understand. *Is this turning of a daughter into a confidante a boundary invasion? Yes, it is!* Sophia's mother completely robbed her daughter of the carefree years of childhood by insisting that Sophia be her (the mother's) companion and confidante. Even as a child, Sophia knew instinctively that she was hearing personal confessions that were inappropriate and far over her head!

"SEX AIN'T MUCH"

"Mother told me all sorts of intimate things I should never have known," Sophia says, "especially not as a child. All the graphic details. She told me things about her childhood and growing up, her strange relationships with her sisters and her parents. She talked about problems with my father, my sister, her sex life. It was pretty terrible.

As far as sex was concerned, I heard the family line. According to my mother, the woman basically takes care of the man's needs. When you are married, that's your responsibility. There was no idea that there could be any joy or even any pleasure in sex. 'It ain't much' was her concept of it. But I was very interested in biology, and it didn't make sense. If there was no pleasure in sex, why did animals procreate or how did the human race perpetuate itself? Sane friends and teachers broadened my outlook, helped me work out my own philosophical outlook.

My father's attitude was healthier. At least it was practical. His idea was that a woman has more to lose than the man and that she has to look after herself. I think he's probably right about that as far as that kind of thinking goes.

My maternal grandfather, as I've said before, had a pathological attitude toward sex or any physical intimacy. My grandmother was a prude who never told my mother the facts of life. She (my mother) had to learn from her six sisters, all of whom were older than she, one of them by almost eighteen years."

LISTENING TO THE INNER VOICE

"I still suffer from a kind of distorted thinking about personal privacy too. Just to illustrate, my son and his girlfriend came home one day when I was taking a nap. The door was closed, and they assumed I wasn't home so they were making love in my son's bedroom. Not realizing they were home, I swung open the door and there they were in a very compromising posture. Instead of being upset with them, I apologized. My son should have made the apologies, but that shows you how skewed I can be."

Sophia had no idea of what it means to be a separate person with distinct boundary lines or how to claim privacy for herself although she recognizes the need in others. And she still questions her own rights to choices in her life. Because of her long history of giving in to a domineering mother and accepting her need for control, it's difficult for her to judge when she should assert herself, when she should be angry. Instinctively, she knows, but her long bout of conditioning has taken its toll.

Sophia would learn very quickly that even though her mother asked for advice, she never listened to a suggestion from anyone. She simply wanted to indulge in self-pity and to fill in her life's many empty spaces. When Mother revealed graphic details of her sex life, it was not because she expected Sophia to counsel her but because she desperately needed a release for her pent-up frustrations. And she had never learned to respect the boundary lines that protect a child from shame and confusion.

"Not only that, but she would ask me to solve a certain dilemma for her," Sophia says, "and then when I would propose a solution—or ten or twelve solutions—she would shoot them all down. I suppose she had to have something left to bother me with the next day. At any rate, if I offered fifteen solutions, she would come up with fifteen reasons why she couldn't do any of them. She still talks to me about her problems, but with the help of 'shrinkage' I now only listen to about 50 percent. That's progress!

I got so I could read things before they happened, a sort of sixth sense or intuition. My sister and I were so busy trying to keep Mother from falling off the edge that we developed these fine antennae like insects. We have an instinct about people. The strange thing is I'm always right about bad vibes. I'm not always right about good ones. In other words, if I pick up bad vibes from a person or an experience, then I can trust my instincts. But sometimes I'm fooled into good vibes from people I shouldn't have put my faith in."

UNCONDITIONAL LOVE: BEWARE!

"I've been zapped royally a few times. A woman I met, a charming woman at first encounter, weaseled her way into my life. I let her befriend me (I don't want to describe all the details—it's too upsetting), and I made a dreadful mistake. She was a major maniac.

Sometimes, in that sense, I give others too much leeway. I'm naturally an understanding, empathetic person, I think, and people take advantage of that. I have a thing about 'unconditional love.' The idea that if you understand people you can love them no matter what. This is okay for husbands or sons or daughters maybe, but you have to watch for it carefully in your relationships with friends. Such a concept can be damaging. Even now I'm thinking about one relationship in which I'm not defending myself very well, and I wonder if I should disengage.

Part of my thinking comes from understanding what my grandparents were like and what they did to my mother. I could justify in that way the terrible things she said to me and did to me. *When people do destructive things, I see it from their perspective, and I don't hold them responsible for their actions.*

Oh, I hold myself responsible, totally responsible. One part of putting up with people who are interesting but difficult is that this helps me to grow in understanding of them and of myself. Somehow I pick people for friends who are creative, exciting but have a 'bug in the craw.' One way or another, I'm still struggling with this, but because of the struggle, I find myself experiencing life on a more complex level.

My whole life experience (or at least childhood and growing-up experience) has been wrestling with demons and intractable problems. At least now I'm dealing with intelligent adults, friends who have lived more fully than my parents ever did. Yet these are still over-protected child-adults stuck in an unhealthy childhood. They have struggled with their feelings of insecurity and anxiety, still are, and since this is what I've always known, I feel comfortable with them. But in not defending myself sometimes, I get exhausted and feel like just pulling the covers over my head. Yet I don't.

The irony is that my ghosts and demons have been emotional food for my art. I think my music is richer for the intensity of all I've been through. And in spite of everything, I think my adult life has been positive. I've made good choices, and though I suspect I may always be wrestling with my personal demons, I've gotten the better of them many times. Certainly by now I'm not a bystander. I'm participating in my life."

TYRANNY IN THE FAMILY SYSTEM: HOW DOES IT HAPPEN?

If we believe, like therapist Jay Haley, that power is central to all human relationships, then it follows logically that the struggle for control is basic to human nature. And since families always arrange themselves into hierarchies, *how much power one person has over another is a central issue in our lives.* Then it also follows that power may be the base of pathology and pathological symptoms the inevitable expression of the struggle.

If a husband controls the family checkbook, for instance, even when the wife is also a breadwinner, he can exert power in many different directions—the lifestyle of the family, what type of car they drive, what kind of vacation, if any, the family takes, the quality of health care the family receives, when and if new clothing is bought. A tremendous number of decisions fall under his domination through the one central core of power—money. And if this man is also domineering and angry, his power may veer into the pathological. He may refuse to allow a necessary operation (such as a mastectomy) because it mars his wife's beauty. Or he may only support his children's education if they follow his choices of a profession. Even with today's atmosphere of feminism and escalation of rights for women, the woman may be regarded as frivolous, extravagant, and lacking in common sense and the man the natural arbiter of the family resources.

But a woman who uses her weaknesses and her feminine resources for manipulation may become an equally powerful figure in the ongoing struggle. Sophia dramatically describes what she so aptly calls "the tyranny of the weak." We discover what happens when family control falls into the hands of the ego-centered woman whose one aim in life is to supply the demands of her own ego, no matter what the sacrifice required of others. Consider Amy, Ellen, and Barbara.

In Amy's case her childlike mother held the reins in her frail but tenacious hands and denied the role she had played in the failure of her marriage or her children's problems. Barbara's mother was so concerned with her own needs that she never asked why her teenage daughter had tried to commit suicide or looked for ways to comfort her. Ellen's mother and Sophia's assumed the position of power by using criticism and unspoken threats of emotional deterioration when their daughters attempted to assert their independence.

THE SURVIVOR—THE RESILIENT CHILD

How do we survive these onslaughts that threaten to destroy our identity, even the very fiber of our being? Sophia tells us,

"I think I was born with a basic kind of strength. I am naturally outgoing and have a fundamental optimism that has carried me through some rough times. Underneath the turmoil there is a strong, healthy personality waiting to emerge.

My sister and I even today have what we call 'reality checks.' We ask each other, 'Am I crazy or is it someone else?' We have a close relationship. I'm lucky because in my mother's family the brothers and sisters were all divided over every issue. My grandmother manipulated them so as to set one against the other.

Mother would say to me, 'No, you don't feel angry (or sad or lonely).' I would say to myself 'she's off the wall. . . . I know what is really going on.' I was constantly trying to stay sane. She would never admit to being wrong although she was very paranoid and always wrestling with ghosts. She could never get beyond that point.

Although I was controlled and manipulated, there was still a part of me that kept its eye on the truth. I kept at things that mattered to me, academics, my music, practicing. I think I basically have a strong personality, a sense of who I am that has enabled me to survive.

Mother supported me as long as I was doing what she wanted. But I was forced to figure out how to take care of her, my father, and myself. I had my music and my support system on the outside, and that kept me whole. But it's never been easy. I'm going to be fifty next month, but I feel much older."

Sophia's life has been, from the beginning, a struggle—a struggle to separate herself from a devouring, needy mother, to find her own identity, to retain her sanity in spite of the pain and loneliness of her family life, to develop her talents as a musician without becoming obsessive and consumed by her disciplined regimen. Yet like Laura, Amy, Ellen, Barbara, Kate, Shelley, and Marie, Sophia is a survivor! She possesses those almost indefinable qualities of hardiness and strength that appear to be the qualities of the *resilient child*—an inborn set of characteristics, which, according to Werner, give the developing child some of the protection she needs. Sophia, like Shelley, was also a *gifted child,* and as Terman discovered in his far-ranging studies of children with outstanding intellectual abilities, such children are often armored with an emotional maturity far beyond their years.

SETTING BOUNDARIES

Yet Sophia even today has problems setting limits in her relationships. She is attracted to people with problems, attractive artistic people, but friends who need her as support. This is what she knows! Even now she is trying to sort out her thinking, wondering if a friend is taking advantage of her. If she continues the relationship as it is, this would be a heavy burden on Sophia's emotional equilibrium, a state difficult for her to maintain. I sensed as she spoke that it was not just one, but many relationships that threaten boundary invasions for Sophia.

And it is difficult for Sophia and for many of us as sensitive, caring human beings to allow our children, our husbands, our friends to suffer, to make mistakes, to learn through painful experience. I think for parents the most agonizing of all decisions is to allow adult children to manage their own lives. When a son or daughter has a problem, we want to "fix" things for him (or her) immediately, to make things right again. It's not just because we love our children deeply, but also because we suffer terribly for and with them. We want to be the knight in shining armor, astride the white horse, who can vanquish all demons and villains. The only problem is, we keep falling off the horse!

We have to allow them to make their own mistakes, to experiment, to fall and pick themselves up again because this is an integral part of the experience of growing up, building character, and developing empathy for others. It's also recognition on our part that we *respect those invisible lines that separate them from us* and allow them to develop into independent, functioning individuals.

On a business level, establishing boundaries and setting limits is a tentative affair. Sophia feels that she has little recourse against an employer who may ask her to work extra hours with no additional compensation or to play through her dinner hour when she desperately needs a break. Since she is both a woman and a musician, she has little power to strike back against unfair or discriminatory arrangements, even a sudden cancellation of an engagement. Musicians' unions, unlike other unionized organizations, offer little protection to their members against the tyrannies of the business world.

UNCONDITIONAL LOVE: A VALID THEORY?

With her husband, Mario, also a gifted musician, Sophia sustains a strong, intuitive relationship, communicating on many levels. They are both emotional beings, subject to wide mood swings of joy and depression, and they have their clear disagreements, but they communicate freely and with a deep underlying sense of trust.

But her perception of "unconditional love," engendered by a long relationship with a pathological parent, makes it doubly difficult for Sophia to assert herself. She feels, as she has in her troubled relationship with her mother, *to know all is to forgive all.* In other words, if she understands the individual's background, the force that have shaped her into eccentric, inconsiderate or demanding ways, then it's possible to accept and love in spite of the pain and hurt that often accompany such a relationship.

Is this a valid theory? Do we have to forgive all because we're aware a person was abused or neglected as a child? Should we overlook behavior that hurts and destroys simply because the perpetrator has suffered damage in the past? Should we pardon a Hitler or a serial killer because he has led an unhappy life? The doctrine of AA—and Christian theology as well—teaches us that when we become adults, *we must begin to assume responsibility for our own lives and actions.*

TAKING RESPONSIBILITY FOR OUR LIVES

Melody Beattie suggests that being responsible means:

1. tending to our own needs—physical, social, emotional, and financial
2. identifying and meeting these needs
3. assuming responsibility for solving our own problems and for making choices in our lives
4. making decisions about our responsibilities to others
5. respecting the rights of others to make their own choices and live up to their responsibilities.

I want to emphasize again that when parents or caregivers have violated our rights with continued physical or sexual or emotional abuse, *we don't have to forgive them.* We can look at them with understanding and at the forces that warped their lives, but we can also hold them accountable! They are responsible for the tremendous hurt and chaos they have caused in our lives. *We do have to forgive ourselves*—we were not the perpetrators; we did not provoke our parents (or grandparents) into the terrible acts they committed; we, as children, were helpless victims. But we do have to resolve our feelings and put these violations behind us, realizing that once we do, we can begin to live our lives without bitterness or blame.

SETTING LIMITS TO MAINTAIN SANITY

Sophia readily admits that even after years of therapy she still struggles with keeping her emotional balance, but she has learned to protect herself for the sake of her sanity and survival. These are the steps that work for her:

1. Step away from the emotional chaos of relationships in the family triangle.
2. "Detach with love"—the AA principle that insists you allow your loved ones to take responsibility for their own actions while still offering love and support.
3. Keep your perspective by listening to your own inner voice and checking out dilemmas with a trusted person.
4. Practice saying "no" until you learn how.
5. Express yourself creatively—through music, art, poetry, gardening, or whatever delights you.

Sophia continues, as do many of us, to wrestle with onslaughts from family and friends. But she has her eye on the truth; the inner eye that sustains her and keeps her sane is always there to help her sort out the real world from fantasy, madness from reason. To maintain their emotional equilibrium, Sophia and her sister still use a system of "reality checks." Talking to each other on the phone almost daily, they check to discover if each is in touch with reality, especially after a draining, frustrating conversation with the mother. "Am I paranoid or is she?" the sisters will ask one another, making certain that neither has drifted off into the mother's surreal world. Then they can laugh, "No, no, she's still crazy. We are not."

Sophia's innate vision and strength have made it possible for her to survive the most complex and painful of situations; she is imbued with a resonance of spirit that enables her to stand outside the emotional intensity of the family and practice detachment with love and affection. Paradoxically, her "demons" have fed her art, her music, her creative life. They are all richer for the conflicts and hardships she has endured.

Sophia has survived the odds. A lovely, gifted woman at fifty, she has emerged from a symbiotic relationship that might have left her crippled, unfulfilled, even mentally ill, to break the chain of pathology. The next two chapters will expand on the ways in which we learn to use strengths, defend our rights, and give ourselves power over our own lives.

> . . . I want to bang my bucket
> with the handle of a spoon,
> I want to stand, Yes Ma'am,
> marching with the faithful,
> Lord, Lord
> fast as I can.
>
> I want to shuffle, prance,
> yes, yes,
> climbing Jacob's ladder,
> stepping onto Glory Land,
> Lord, Lord, let me dance!
>
> —"I Don't Want to Be a Presbyterian"

8

Bur and Honey

... A red-winged blackbird
zips to the height
of a dying cypress,
preening black satin feathers,
scarlet stripes, praising
the contrast of fire and dust,
life and death.
If this hour is gliding
out from under,
darkness drifting in like feathers,
winged and sly,
I want to pour this day
into my life,
bur and honey, green and ripe.

—"Bur and Honey"

Susan is a tall, willowy brunette in her late twenties. Dressed in
shorts and a T-shirt, wearing no makeup, she could be a teenager
on her way to the gym; in a floppy straw hat and a long flowered
skirt she is a free spirited bohemian, stopping to talk animatedly
with friends; in an expensive silk suit she looks the part of the ad-
vertising executive she once was, en route to a business meeting
with a client.

But Susan has had to struggle with deep-seated feelings of abandonment to achieve her hard-earned composure. She has had to over-

come enormous odds simply to survive in a world where chaos threatened many times.

GROWING UP TOO SOON

"In many ways I was a little adult," Susan says sadly. "My sister, brother, and I were never allowed to spend a lot of time playing and having fun. With Mom it was cut and dried. There was a lot to be done, and we had a full list of chores and projects on weekends. Sometimes we could go down to the basement and play games, but the time we spent with Mom was serious.

We took on duties, all of us, as soon as we were able. I had definite assignments from the time I was five. Mom was a school principal, and this was the only way she could manage. In the mornings, before we left for school, my brother would vacuum, my sister Joan would do the dishes, and my job was to clean the bathrooms.

On nice days we rode our bikes to school. My brother, Bobby, who was eleven (six years older than I), would be in charge, and he really tried to look after us. It was a big responsibility for him, but Mom knew she could trust him completely. He would never leave us on that long ride to school, and he gave us a lot of encouragement whenever we were discouraged and lagged behind.

I did a lot of things early. I started first grade when I was five. I learned to ride a bike when I was five. I was always expected to keep up. When you have older siblings, you tend to do things earlier, and I was highly motivated to follow them.

My physical needs were taken care of, but my life was a lot stricter than anyone else's. We weren't allowed to watch TV except for a few selected programs or to read comic books or to eat cookies and candy. We were strictly regimented, which may have come from Mom being a teacher."

SURVIVING THE ODDS

"My defenses sprang into action at an early age," Susan recalls. "I think it was because I saw my brother and sister testing Mom's limits and what happened when they resisted her. She exploded when they tried to go against her, and I knew that method wasn't for me. My defense was to hide and sleep. There would be a dinner party, the house to be cleaned and the table set for twelve, and I couldn't handle it. I would hide so I couldn't be found and then drop off to sleep.

I've always been able to sleep anywhere, anytime. If I needed sleep, Mom understood that because so did she, and it was okay. It was how I got her physical affection too. I would go in and sleep with her and Dad when I was a little girl, and that was the only time she could relax and show affection. It seems to me Dad was gone a lot. When he was there, he pretty much went along with what Mom wanted although he was a more caring, demonstrative person. I remember how he used to spend hours with me in the park and with my younger cousin, Joel, swinging us high on the swings and catching us with a hug when we came down the slides.

SUSAN: THE PARENTAL CHILD

Susan clearly exemplifies the "parental child," the child who is never allowed her childhood. Very early she was pushed toward adulthood and the responsibilities of that role. She started first grade a year early and took on household responsibilities "as soon as she could manage them." If there was company coming, Susan and her sister, Joan, were to make sure the downstairs was dusted and in order, the table set, toys and books put up. Then they might be sent to bed before the guests arrived!

A marriage of two incompatible people often produces a vacuum and results in cross-generational reversal of roles and boundary invasion. Since there is little intimacy between the marital partners, the husband may turn to his work to fill the relationship vacuum, and the wife may turn to a child to bring her a sense of fulfillment and to assuage her loneliness. The generational crossover builds strong ties between parent and child that violate generational boundaries—those invisible border lines necessary for building a sense of identification.

Confusion erupts when we reverse the generations. The cross-generational reversal of roles is dramatically illustrated by Laura, Ellen, Amy, Shelley, Barbara, and Susan. In families like these there's no time for being a child, for Mom needs a partner—a partner she can control. Dad needs someone to take Mom's focus from him and allow him to distance himself from the unhappy marital relationship. Yet Susan, at the same time that she was expected to shoulder adult responsibilities, found that Mom was still very much in charge and no one was *ever* to deviate from her decisions.

There was little time for fun and games as Mom believed that no time should be wasted in frivolous pursuits. Even games were pursued with the aim of learning a skill or strategy—and maybe even becoming a champion! Susan was always expected "to keep up" with her siblings at the pace Mom set for her.

BIRTH ORDER AND THE FAMILY ROLE

Several fascinating studies have shown that birth order may be linked with personality characteristics as well as levels of achievement in later life. Firstborn children, for example, are expected to achieve at higher levels than their younger siblings. Their language skills develop sooner and are more complex, but firstborns are often the victims of more intrusive and restrictive parental attitudes. Although they may receive more attention than later-born children, they are also subjected to more punishment and stricter discipline as well as child rearing practices that are less skilled and less confident.

Mom didn't expect as much of Susan, the baby of the family, as she did from Bobby or Joan, and Susan was the descending *angel*, a beautiful, curly-haired baby who was undemanding, easy-going, and happy. In addition, Susan's survival mechanism was an unconscious protective response that stood her in good stead as a defense from Mom's demands. She could sleep anywhere, anytime, and although she would hear Mom calling for her from a long way off, she was safe, knowing that Mom valued sleep and wouldn't interrupt her. Susan's method was *passive resistance* since not only was this her natural mode of response but also because she had seen the explosion of Mom's temper when her sister or brother rebelled. And she had found that open resistance didn't work anyway as Mom always prevailed in the long run.

We don't hear a lot about Dad in Susan's story except that he was "away a lot" of the time. When he was around, Susan could turn to him for affection and support, and his loving presence may account in part for Susan's strength today. Yet he probably had little say in family decisions or plans. There was never any question as to the power base in the family, and Susan accepted early that Mom determined the course of action and there was no point in struggling against the tide.

How did this process affect Susan? You can be sure it made for a lot of insecurity and confusion. She was expected to be independent and self-sufficient and yet was never consulted as to decisions that affected her life dramatically. As she grew into adulthood, she found it hard to understand why it was so difficult for her to make even small decisions on her own. It wasn't until much later when she was living away from her home and totally independent that she realized that, although much was demanded of her in the way of competence, intelligence, and achievement, she had never had to make judgments and choices on her own!

Susan says, "I didn't keep a diary. I never liked to read and write. Even though Mom pushed us to excel in school, I wasn't encouraged to think creatively or to express myself. That's why I'm happy that Brian (my son) likes storytelling. He can express himself so imaginatively and freely because he's been brought up that way. I always considered writing a chore.

I never had many friends growing up except for kids in the neighborhood. I seldom brought a friend home from school because we were always so busy, and Mom didn't allow us to visit friends for sleeping overnight. She didn't feel comfortable with us staying with someone else where she didn't have control over what went on.

In fact, I don't recall ever bringing problems to Mom. There was no energy left for that. We had to get things done—housework or homework or practicing piano or tennis or whatever. She was very goal-oriented. I kept to myself. I don't remember talking to anyone else either about what I felt. Mom wasn't comfortable with feelings at any rate. There was never any time, and I think it made her uncomfortable to say she loved us or to give us a hug. Even now at age sixty she is barely able to say anything remotely related to feelings.

And if we tried telling her of a disappointment or frustration, she would argue that our feelings didn't really exist—we were being overly dramatic or exaggerating or being a baby. When I was angry or couldn't have something I wanted, Dad could deal with it more easily, but he didn't get involved in arguments or confrontations if he could help it.

My brother, Bobby, used to have temper tantrums, and I don't think any of us ever considered what might have provoked them. When he would jump around the living room in one of his fits, Mom would make a joke of it and say, 'Let's all jump too, follow Bobby around the room.' That was her way of dealing with it. We never tried to figure what was making him so upset.

My brother kept to himself, to his Hardy Boy books and his dog or hamster. He loved animals from the time he was a little boy and brought home all the strays. My sister, Joan, and I could talk about things to some extent but not with my brother. Unfortunately, I think

Joan was always jealous of me. She thought I was prettier because my looks were so different from hers; I was tall and brown-eyed, she was short and blue-eyed. She thought she was 'fat' because she had a few feminine curves whereas I had none; I was built like a boy until I was in my teens. She didn't think of herself as being attractive even though she definitely was—as a little girl and an adolescent. And Mom wanted us each to have our separate areas of expertise. Joan liked music so I stopped taking piano lessons and concentrated on tennis so we wouldn't have to compete.

The jealousy between Joan and me may have started early because I was the baby. My brother was a difficult child and Joan less so, but I was an 'angel.' Such a good baby. I never cried, just ate and slept, ate and slept. Then they discovered when I was eighteen months old that I was almost totally deaf! I had some sort of inner ear fungus that they took care of as soon as they discovered the problem, but those first months I didn't hear a thing. It was a blessing in a way. 'God works in mysterious ways,' you know. With three babies and Mom's ambitions, all she needed was a demanding baby. I was insulated from the world with my deafness, Mom's perfect little infant, always so placid and so good.

Mom ran her household like a ship, everything tight and clean and orderly. We were always so busy there was never any time for reflecting, for figuring out what direction you wanted to take. I'm just now starting to realize you don't have to be constantly achieving things."

THE AUTHORITARIAN HOUSEHOLD

Research, based primarily on the studies of Diana Baumrind, has shown that children growing up in *authoritarian families*—who are demanding and controlling and show little warmth or closeness—often have lower self-esteem and are less socially adaptable than their peers. These are families with rigid individual boundaries, whose focus is on achievement and accomplishments rather than on building ties of love and understanding. Sometimes children of such families are subdued and passive; often they demonstrate aggressive or even rebellious behavior. Psychologist Gerald Patterson found that the aggressive child, who is out of control, is likely to come from a family in which parents are authoritarian but lack the skills to enforce strict rules.

Children growing up in *permissive* homes find few rules or patterns to live by. There is warmth and affection between family members, but these children are often aggressive and immature in their inter-actions with peers and in school because they have never learned to respect the rights of others or to defer to authority.

The most negative outcome of all the types of child rearing, ac-cording to the experts, evolves from the *neglectful* family pattern, where the child's basic emotional and physical nurturing needs are ignored or denied. Such children don't relate well to other children or to their peers and are likely to demonstrate antisocial or even disturbed behavior, especially in adolescence, and many of these effects con-tinue well into adulthood.

On the other hand, consistent positive behavior is associated with the *authoritative parent who sets clear and understandable limits but is also warm and responsive.* Children growing up in such families usually show a higher level of self esteem, are more independent, more generous, and more concerned with the welfare of others than their peers and are self-confident and academically more successful.

Susan's family has all the earmarks of the *authoritarian pattern.* Susan's family lived by a strict regimen set by Mom, who was deter-mined that her children should have the things she never had—a spacious house, handsome furniture, a piano, tennis, and dancing lessons. But this goal was impossible for her to achieve alone so every member of the family was actively involved, working at projects around the house, keeping up with academics, and pursuing an avocation such as tennis or dancing.

THE BIG QUESTION: DOES ANYONE CARE?

"We were all pushed out very early," Susan recalls. "Joan and Bobby went off to boarding school when they were still in their early teens and so did I. Bobby even spent a year in Switzerland with a former tutor when he was only twelve or thirteen!

When I started to play tennis at around eleven or twelve, it was very difficult. I would get up at 5:00 A.M. and Mom would drop me off to practice at the courts, then she would pick me up for school. I felt as though I stood out from everyone else on the tennis courts just as I did in school. Mom wouldn't let me wear the white tennis skirts and shorts that everyone else did—she made mine! And I wore boys' sneak-ers because in those days they didn't offer anything but Keds for girls. I even tried wearing nurses' shoes to give me some support. And I had these huge feet.

We were constantly traveling around to tennis matches, and I get car sick easily so we would have to stop along the way for me to recoup. After a while I just couldn't take it. Physically or otherwise. I got dehydrated from the strenuous tennis sessions and was terribly sick. But Mom thought after I recovered that I should still play. I just couldn't. I knew instinctively that I wasn't up to it.

That summer I quit playing tennis I wanted to learn Spanish so I could go to Mexico on an exchange scholarship for the next year. But Mom said I couldn't unless I agreed to play tennis. I was about fifteen.

This was my first bang-up confrontation with her, and we had an awful explosion. But this was only the beginning!

I still have huge conflicts and ambivalence in my relationship with Mom. When she told me on the phone just recently that she missed me, I was so happy. I couldn't believe it. I had never been sure how much she cared."

THE RIGID FAMILY SYSTEM: ISOLATION AND LONELINESS

Families with rigid external boundaries allow very little interaction with the outside world, and although she was given the very best education and went to wonderful schools, Susan never felt as if she belonged. Because Mom was the principal of her school, she and her sister and brother felt set apart from the rest of the students. "I always felt different, never part of the group," Susan says, "because we really were different. Mom had great ambitions for us and for herself too, I think."

Throughout Susan's childhood and adolescence it was a struggle for the family to fit into the wealthy lifestyle of the suburb where they lived. Both parents worked and though they enjoyed a comfortable income, it was never enough for the luxuries that neighbors or friends enjoyed. Sometimes it was barely enough to maintain such a lifestyle!

Susan's sense of isolation was further heightened by all-consuming activities that set her apart from her peers—early morning tennis practice, long drives to tennis matches, the battle to keep up academically. Only the highest level of achievement was acceptable to Mom in every area. Even when she played tennis Susan felt alien and isolated. She couldn't wear the elegant white skirts and shorts that were a "uniform" for the other girls—her clothes were stitched by Mom to save money.

No matter how troubled Susan might be (or her sister and brother), real feelings were seldom expressed in this rigid family that lacked any idea of how to communicate with one another.

REVERSING GENERATIONAL ROLES: BECOMING A PARENT'S CONFIDANTE

Jay Haley along with Selvini Palazzoli and her colleagues, rather than looking for causes for individual problems, see families as involved in "games" that maintain the *homeostasis*—or equilibrium—of the family system. Healthy, flexible families grow and adapt, but rigid families get into trouble because they are more concerned with the stability of the system than adapting to changing circumstances. Family players are stuck in a rigid sequence of rules that are no longer functional, but they are determined for the system to survive and expend tremendous energy in resisting influences that might force them to change.

Susan was drawn into the family game as her parents' conflict became more intense. She recognizes now that her mother and father were alienated from each other for a long time before the actual separation and divorce, that they were living in separate wings of the house with separate lives in an atmosphere of distrust and bitterness—although there was little overt expression of the hidden dissension between them. When her parents did make the decision to separate, both her older brother and sister were away at school; she had few ties to friends or other relatives, and she felt isolated and lonely.

Suddenly at eleven or twelve, still struggling with her own feelings of loneliness and alienation, Susan became the unwilling confidante for both parents' woes. Susan, looking wistful, says softly, "They both told me their problems and I was not to tell the other one. Mom was having an affair with a man she'd known for a while; there may have been more than one affair. I was thirteen when they separated, but things must have started up earlier when I was eleven or even sooner. My brother and sister, whom I'd always relied on to take care of me, were both away then at private boarding school. I was in never-never land, neither woman nor child."

THE FAMILY SCENE: CONFLICTS AND COALITIONS

Susan's story is a dramatic one, drawing us into the emotional intensity of a compelling narrative—a talented, driven mother who controls the household; the unseen conflict between the parents; a series of triangulations as each child is drawn into the foray; Susan's struggle for survival.

Susan became the focus of the family triangle as her parents drew further and further apart. Since her older brother and sister were away at boarding schools, Susan was left to relieve the anger and anxiety of both mother and father. Invading the cross-generational boundary between parent and child, each parent tried to draw her into an *alliance* against the other. We see this happening time and time again in dysfunctional families, where the child is not only expected to take on an adult role but is expected to actively side with one parent against the other, especially at times of stress like death or divorce. According to Minuchin, one of the first steps in counseling unhappy households like Susan's is the *setting of generational boundaries* so that parents deal with problems directly instead of turning the whole family into a battleground!

Behind the scenes in Susan's family, Mom propelled each member forward to achieve ambitious goals. Susan was to become a champion tennis player, her sister Joan a musician, her serious brother a scholar. We can point to endless triangulations and coalitions as the process of estrangement and separation begins between the parents—Mom and Susan allied against Dad; Mom and Susan, Joan, and Bobby allied against Dad; Susan taking sides with Dad against Mom; each child being pulled in a different direction without any real understanding of what is going on. And there was even rivalry between the two sisters, Mom siding with Joan and Susan isolated at the other end of the triangle.

SUSAN'S WORLD TURNS INSIDE OUT

Susan explains, "When I was fifteen, things really erupted. I was in love, or thought I was, with a boy who had been Joan's friend, and when we started dating, she got furiously jealous, claiming I had stolen her boyfriend even though they had only dated a few times! That was one of the most miserable summers of my life, looking in from the outside all the time and Mom and Joan both angry with me— Mom because I wouldn't play tennis any longer and Joan because I was dating her former boyfriend.

"After that summer it all happened so fast," Susan relates, amazed even now at the turn her life took then. "The young girls from Spain came over to live with us on one of those foreign exchange programs and I went back with them. When I came back my grandmother (Mom's mother) had died of a heart attack, Mom and Dad had divorced, Mom had remarried, and we were living in another state. All this happened between August and December of that year. Whoa! I couldn't believe it. My life had turned inside out, and no one had bothered to inform me or tried to prepare me in any way.

When I came back, I was living in a strange house and all of my possessions had totally disappeared. My furniture, books, everything! I never knew what happened to them. Suddenly I had two stepsisters and was sharing a room with one of them. We are great friends now, but I barely knew her name then. Mom had decided, without consulting any of us, that it would be a good idea to split the sisters up. And I was living in my stepsister's space. There was no evidence of anything of mine.

Then another big change—I had always gone to private school, and now I was enrolled in a big public high school where I didn't fit in. My clothes and my background were different. I didn't know anything about clothes because I had always worn a uniform."

BOUNDARY INVASIONS: THEY CAUSE LONG-LASTING TRAUMA

Susan suffered *boundary invasions* throughout childhood and adolescence on a major scale. While she was abroad in Spain, her parents divorced, her mother remarried, and the family had moved to a new home. The whole family scene, as she knew it, had exploded into chaos, blowing each member in different directions. All of this had occurred without any real communication as to what was happening—Mom made the moves and that was that!

Susan's sense of loneliness and isolation that had persisted throughout her life was further heightened now that she was living in a stranger's house, even a stranger's room! In addition, instead of the small private schools she had known all of her life, she was thrust into the chaos of a huge public high school.

Susan's very identity was threatened with the *loss of a father, a grandmother, a home, and a school.* Even her books and furniture, all of her possessions, had disappeared as completely as if an earthquake or hurricane had moved through, swallowing all traces of her former life. And Mom had made all the decisions, as she usually did, without consulting her children or even letting them know what was happening. There was an occasional note to Susan in Madrid, but always brief and dismissive without any real discussion of the emotional upheaval that was breaking up the family. Although the family pattern had been far from perfect, it was at least familiar. It's not surprising that Susan, Joan, and Bobby felt alienated and anxious.

ABANDONMENT: FEAR BECOMES A REALITY

"Then the year after that, I was very happy to go off to boarding school again," Susan continues. " I loved it there until my junior year when everything blew up. Mom called and said my stepfather had lost his business and there would be no money for boarding school next year. She asked if I could possibly finish up in one year even though it was only my junior year, and I tried, but there was no way I could get around the four year requirements for English and religion.

After that financial blow, without consulting with any of us, Mom and my stepfather decided to sell the big house where we lived and move to the city to a studio apartment. We were all on our own, sink or swim then, my brother, sister, and I, plus my stepsisters and one stepbrother. There was no money to send any of us off to college, and unfortunately we were all at college age except for me. I still had another year of high school to go.

I ended up living that summer with a guy who was twenty-six. Let's see—I was either sixteen or seventeen. I wasn't ready for that, but what choice did I have? This particular man had seen me a couple of times and liked me. I didn't even know him. I wasn't angry then, although some of my friends were angry for me. These were great friends who have been a support for me all along. I felt lost and afraid, but I didn't know enough to be angry. I was just following Mom's directives as usual."

THE ATTACHMENT PROCESS: IT STARTS EARLY

One of the child's greatest fears is the *fear of abandonment,* and even as a confident, successful young woman, Susan still struggles with feelings of insecurity and abandonment. As we've seen again and again— with Laura, Ellen, Amy, Shelley, Kate, Barbara, Marie, and Sophia— we desperately need to know that a parent or caregiver loves us and will always be there for us. When this vital element is missing in childhood, we continue the search into adulthood. We are always looking for a husband, lover, friend, even a child, to take care of us, fostering an unhealthy, dependent relationship to fill in the missing link.

A child who feels a sense of sure attachment to the mother can allow the mother to separate from her, confident in the knowledge that she will return. Even as a toddler she feels free to wander away because she believes that the mother will always be there for her. Parents of secure babies are emotionally expressive. They smile, laugh, talk to the baby, and hold her. She, in turn, responds by smiling, cooing, gesturing toward the mother.

Mothers of insecure children are often emotionally unavailable. They may be "needy" women, like Susan's or Amy's mothers, who are too closely wrapped up in their own needs to give affection or warmth to their offspring. Or they may suffer from addiction or depression. Mothers like this don't want physical contact with their babies, and, not surprisingly, these babies, as they grow up, avoid physical contact with others because they are uncomfortable with any display of affection or demonstrativeness.

The studies of Mahler, Bowlby, and Ainsworth have demonstrated that children with secure attachments tend to be emotionally healthier in almost every way. They form more lasting relationships with friends and are better at solving problems. In addition, these children seem to be able to cope with stress much more successfully, as a secure sense of self shields them against the complexities and hardships of later life.

However, the good news is that, as important as the first attachment is, children can recover from an insecure childhood, if they receive that nurturing elsewhere—from a grandparent, an older sibling, a stepparent, even a teacher. And we do find individuals who appear to defy all categories; psychologists think of her as the *resilient* child. Look at Ellen, now an outgoing, creative adult, whose mother and father were cold and unresponsive, who held their only daughter responsible for all the conflicts between them and for their unhappy lives together. Or consider Shelley, the brilliant author, teacher, and lawyer, who lived a completely neglected childhood—or the talented essayist and poet, Barbara, whose childhood was traumatic and painful. There is Amy, growing up with a neurotic, childlike mother and a distant father, who today is a strong, compassionate young woman.

In each case we can trace some nurturing influence. Ellen's Norwegian grandparents were noisy, articulate, and loving although her grandmother died when Ellen was only seven and her parents moved away. Barbara became very close to an elementary school friend and her affectionate, expressive family and spent many happy hours with them. Although she didn't want to disturb them with a sense of her small family's growing alienation, Amy's grandparents were caring and nurturing. Shelley found remarkable teachers who opened vistas for her. And Susan's father, though never authoritative or the decision maker in the household, was a caring person who continues to give his daughter love and encouragement.

SUSAN SHOWS HER METTLE, BUT IT'S FRIGHTENING OUT THERE!

"That arrangement with a boyfriend didn't last long of course," Susan relates, "and I moved out and found a college that would take me despite my never having finished high school. I had $100 a month to live on so I moved into a cold water flat with tin over the windows. It was actually an abandoned building, but I could live there rent-free if I promised to do some renovating for the landlord. Also I managed to get a tennis scholarship and made my way into the honors program in the college where there was some academic challenge. I was the 'token WASP' in an urban school composed of city kids, minority groups, and handicapped students who were bright and ambitious.

I wasn't scared living in this desolate building until later on when someone broke in and stole everything. But I had to work to live there. I tiled the floors, put in kitchen counters, painted and papered. I couldn't afford to buy books so I borrowed them or read my homework in the library. I was also working in a real estate office, modeling, and helping handicapped students to take notes. The latter was a volunteer job that meant taking notes for every class, but it helped me too as I never missed a class. I couldn't because the students depended on me, and that was what pulled me through—I would cram for exams plus taking notes in class. There wasn't much time for studying otherwise."

INDEPENDENCE AND CONTROL

How do we teach a child competence and independence? The experts say we should start early by giving the toddler small choices, asking her which toy she likes, or her preference for a flavor of ice cream, for example. Then choices can be enlarged as the child begins to grows up. We can give her choices in the clothes she wears to school (as long as they are appropriate); she can help us decide which TV program to watch, which color to paint her room. She will soon start to make decisions on her own—her friends, the sports or activities she prefers, the stories or books she reads.

We also teach the child independence by our actions—by modeling. If we are willing to learn and to grow, to take risks by skiing a new trail or by taking beginner piano lessons or going back to graduate school, then our daughters and sons have a model for courage and independent thinking. If we express our ideas on issues of the day, if we read and are aware of happenings on the political and international scene, in the arts, then we also give our children a model for expanding their lives through learning and research.

Psychological research shows that as we encourage the child to make her own decisions, we should also offer guidance when and if it's needed. But once she is informed, we allow her to reason for herself and make the final choice. In the process we build confidence and self-esteem—that she is a competent, responsible person who can make wise judgments. As she takes on more complex projects in early adolescence, we can offer praise and demonstrate our love and respect for her even in cases where a decision turns out to be a faulty one. After all, the only way we can learn is by doing, and when we are afraid to attempt something new, we fail before we even start!

But when we try to *control* another person's life—whether child, husband, or friend—then we run into trouble. Because the need to control ends up controlling us and becoming the center of our lives. And this is a frustrating, ultimately defeating goal as we can't control anything in our lives except our own behavior.

We see this in Susan's experience as her mother tries to fashion her into a tennis champion. There was tremendous conflict between Mom and Susan when Susan realized that, physically and emotionally, the life of a professional athlete was not for her. Susan's sister, Joan, seldom outwardly rebelled against Mom either, but in her college years she turned to drugs and alcohol as a way of relieving the pain and anxiety she felt.

Mom may have believed that she was teaching her children and stepchildren independence when she suddenly sold their spacious home and informed them that they were on their own and could *sink or swim*. But even in times of crisis we can't teach confidence and independence by suddenly dropping our children overboard. They may drown! And Susan could easily have drowned—becoming a petty criminal, a drug addict, or a psychotic.

What could Susan's Mom and stepfather have done to resolve their difficult situation? They might have communicated openly with their children, discussing all the pros and cons of a number of solutions (i.e., moving to a smaller house; or each family member taking on extra jobs or working part-time until the crisis had eased; or even taking out a loan). The point is that it was possible to work out a solution together, with each family member suggesting a possible response and being willing to make a sacrifice for the sake of the family if necessary.

Several studies of group dynamics indicate that cohesiveness and compatability make for a well-functioning family unit. Such a family has complementary aims that not only work for the achievements of the group as a whole but also take into account varying individual needs. The family develops patterns for handling conflicts and disagreements and operates flexibly so that new methods of accommodation can be found when there is a shift in circumstances.

The dichotomy in Susan's family was that Mom had taught her children well—they were industrious, skilled, and competent. Certainly Susan was. She could refinish kitchen cabinets, rewire electrical circuits, and fix the plumbing. She could live on a $100 a month in a deserted building, pay the rent, keep up her schoolwork, and tutor handicapped students. Yet, in spite of all of her capabilities, Susan never felt she could trust her own judgment. Mom had always been in control!

As in many unhealthy family systems, individual boundaries were rigid, and the emphasis was on independence at the expense of affection and close bonding between members. But Susan's relationship with Mom was ultimately a dependent one, with roles and responsibilities of the two generations inextricably intertwined. Mom, who had felt deprived during her own chaotic and financially insecure childhood, often played the role of the child as her daughters and son scurried around doing the household chores. Mom longed to be a girl again, with someone to take care of her.

CHAOS THREATENS

"In the middle of my second year," Susan says matter-of-factly, "the place where I lived was robbed and vandalized. I was visiting with

Mom in her little apartment over Christmas, and the boiler shut down and flooded my building. Somebody broke in, and it was a huge mess. They stole shoes, suitcases, Mom's sterling, everything, the TV, the stereo, even the garbage cans.

I wasn't angry at the time all this was happening. Again, I remember friends being angry for me. I accepted the situation for what it was and was too busy surviving to think about the ramifications. I think I was too stunned to feel anything.

The worst part was that the ceiling fell in on my papers, and I had to take an incomplete in all of my courses. When I had to make up the papers and exams, I had forgotten a lot of what I knew, and naturally my grades were not as good as they would have been, mostly 'C's,' I think. I was beginning to have these terrible headaches like red hot explosions in my head, and I didn't know why. I must have repressed everything!

I couldn't go back to live in that building after that. I just couldn't face it, but the landlord let me live in another apartment of his that didn't require any work. I had done a lot for him in the other place, and he was still able to resurrect it later on. I loved this little place. It was perfect—in a nice neighborhood and easy to keep up. I was as happy as I had been as a little kid."

SUSAN SURVIVES—DESPITE THE ODDS!

"There was never any question of being able to go off somewhere to school," Susan relates. "I would have liked that, the proms and dating college fraternity boys, living in the dorms, all of that. However, I was an honor student and graduated with a 3.5 average. I made up my mind I wanted to go to law school so that the things that had happened to me could never happen to my children. I knew by then that if I didn't take care of myself, no one else would.

I had trouble getting into law school, though, because my reading skills have never been great and my LSAT scores were not impressive. Dad drove me up finally to a school in New England, and I talked my way into an interview. When the admissions counselor heard my story, she was absolutely blown away. They accepted me a few weeks later. I took out a student loan and Dad made up the difference.

I worked in the summers to make money. I used books in the library rather than buying them and I lived basically on bagels. Law school was hard work, but I made a few friends—only two continuing friendships. These were people I lived with there, a couple with small children. I found time to run a variety show too.

All that time during law school I had a boyfriend who lived in Vermont. We split up when I finished school. We had different goals. I wanted to achieve, and I think he was jealous of me. He was finishing undergraduate school and wasn't sure where he was headed, and I was finishing law school.

I came to New York and lived with Mom and my stepfather in their one-bedroom apartment. I slept on the couch. For about a year-and-a half I lived there and helped Mom run her art gallery. I totally organized the business and worked in the office from eight until six, then came home to the apartment and stocked it with food. I lived rent-free but wasn't receiving any commission for what I sold.

I was also studying for the Bar and took it in January. But there was no time to study or review. Naturally I failed it. I took the exam again after that and took two weeks off to review. I needed two months. I was pretty devastated though when I failed again. I was still running the office, and there just wasn't enough preparation time. The following winter I met W., and we were engaged very fast after that and married in September. He has always thought of me as Cinderella and he the prince who rescued me.

Mom never made allowances for the commissions I earned. Her partner finally paid me back though. She thinks I'm talented artistically and as a business manager and wants me to come back into the business."

FORGIVENESS: A PART OF GROWING UP

"You have to understand Mom's background to realize why she was so determined to make it—why she felt that being successful and achieving your goals were the only things that counted. She had a difficult childhood. Her parents were incompatible, her father was crippled and brought up on a farm where everyone worked, believed in the value of hard work with none of the frills. Both her parents were teachers, and in those days teachers made very little money.

Her mother loved music, art, drama, dance, but they were always pinched for money so that she worked long hours and was seldom home. Mom never had the chance to learn piano or take ballet lessons so she was determined that we would have all the opportunities she had missed. Like her mother, she was always running from one thing to another to provide all these special things for us—although we had more money and a lot greater opportunities were there for us.

THE FAMILY HERITAGE: A LEGACY OF CONFLICT

Susan's Mom grew up in a unhappy household where her parents were in violent disagreement over family finances, discipline, and even the lifestyle they wanted for themselves and their children, in a home where money was scarce and where there were constant arguments over how it should be apportioned. Susan now can look at her mother compassionately, understanding why she was so relentless in the pursuit of her goal to achieve, become a success, be constantly admired.

Her mother's parents (Susan's grandparents) were basically incompatible spirits, the grandfather a practical, gruff man embittered by a restrictive childhood and a progressive disease that left him crippled. Her grandmother, growing up a poverty stricken Scottish family, yearned for paintings, books, and outings at the theater or ballet. Her grandparents separated when their two older children were in high school, the younger brother still a small boy, and though they never actually divorced, feelings of anger and bitterness ran high.

Susan's Mom, in turn, was determined that her children would have a better life. But the better life meant for her going back to school for a graduate degree, beginning a career when her children were still small, spending every waking moment planning, scraping, scheming, and working. Because she had known little nurturing from her busy, unhappy parents, she unwittingly followed the same pattern, equating the time she spent teaching her children and working with them as an expression of love.

Susan's mom was uncomfortable with any expression of feeling or with resolving issues by delving to find the root of the problem. In order to keep feelings well-buried and to achieve her pressing goals, she stayed busy, busy, busy. There was never time for reflection or for openly discussing grievances. She taught, played racquetball, renovated the bathroom, refinished an antique chest.

Mom had no model for giving her children the kind of loving, nurturing environment they needed. Instead she substituted a work-oriented pattern in which every member of the family was an active participant. In her own way her mother loved them, Susan thinks, but Mom believed the only way she and her children could succeed was by developing skills, competency, coming out on top. And Mom believed strongly that only *she* was capable of making the right decision for their future well-being.

Of course when strong emotions are involved—as they are always are at times of separation, divorce, and remarriage—it's difficult to make rational decisions. And Susan's Mom had never been gifted with either empathy or insight. She was a needy person whose life centered around her own wants and interests.

RELATIONSHIPS: MAINTAINING BALANCE

"When I think back on it," Susan says, "I had a void for a long time. I didn't have close friends in grammar school or high school. There was no time in the schedule for friendships. My first cousin who is two years younger was my closest friend growing up. He still is although now I've begun now to form some wonderful, compatible relationships with a lot of give and take. I was off at boarding school for two years, and then that came to an abrupt end so I didn't get a chance to pursue those attachments, and they were severed. I made three friends in college who have stood by me through all the rough times. I'm still close to them today.

My friendships in law school were pretty one-sided. I did all the giving. My roommate got involved in an affair with a college professor and was a 'user' too so that relationship didn't amount to much. I seemed to always get involved then with people who took advantage of me. That may have been because I looked for people who were needy so I could be the caretaker and resolve their problems. That was what I knew, taking care of other people. There was a pretty steady pattern of that. Another friend was also a user, a drug user, that is. I helped her to survive, get an apartment. I lent her money, and when she went to Europe a few years ago, she never even tried to get in touch with me after she came back.

A friendship developed with a guy who was producing a film. He stayed with my husband and me in our apartment. I encouraged him, lent him money, the whole works because I could see he was a needy person. Suddenly I started to realize he never offered anything in return, never even called most of the time to say thank you or how are you.

I didn't have any model for relationships. My grandmother and grandfather (Mom's parents) were separated for years, and Dad's parents died a long time ago. There was no relationship between my parents for ages before they separated. There was no love. They didn't share a bedroom or show any signs of affection. I didn't have a clue as to how that works. I must have had an instinct for it though because look at the wonderful man I chose for a husband.

Because of the way I was brought up I thought all friendships were based on need. My husband has a huge number of friends that date back to his childhood and he can't understand why I don't, but Mom didn't have a circle of friends either. There was no time for that. Except for my college friends, I am just starting to make real friends, friends who care about the same things I do and like the same things. Now I have relationships where my friends give me support and I give them love and understanding in return. I think, too, I used to be very critical of people. I was hard on myself too."

Bandura argues that social behaviors are learning through modeling—through watching how others behave. Thus the child who watches a parents behave in generous, compassionate ways—taking care of a sick friend, giving of time and energy to help others—will learn generous and thoughtful behavior. What children learn from reinforcement of positive behavior and through modeling is not just behavior but ideas, perceptions, internal standards, and self-concept. These beliefs and expectations form the core of the developing personality and affect behavior in consistent and enduring ways. The child who sees a parent behave in rude or violent ways often learns anger and violence as a way of resolving problems and develops a negative core of beliefs and expectations.

Although the conflict between her parents was covert and seldom openly expressed, Susan had few patterns for loving relationships. She saw little affection demonstrated between her parents; her father's father was dead and his mother elderly; and her mother's parents were separated, had been for years. Her relationship with her sister, though close and loving, was marred by rivalry and jealousy, and her brother withdrew into his own separate world. Almost her only constant friendship as she was growing up was with her first cousin, J., two years younger than she.

In the few friendships Susan established in law school, relationships were based, not on shared interests or values, but on taking care of others. She reached out to people who needed her support because she felt at this point that she would be valued only on the basis of what she could give! She often felt let down when there was no reciprocal giving, but as her friends were often "damaged" people, suffering from terrible childhoods, Susan felt it was up to her to supply what they needed. There is a strong parallel between Susan's premise for relationships and Sophia's theory of "unconditional love," which means that we can forgive our friends their weaknesses once we understand the painful experiences that have molded them. But just as Sophia is beginning to doubt the validity of her thinking, Susan realizes now that there should be give and take in relationships, and the friends she chooses now want to share her triumph and grief, want to give back the understanding and support she offers them.

MOVING TOWARD INDEPENDENCE: IT'S NEVER EASY

"Sometimes when I wonder why I get so easily depressed," Susan says reflectively, "I remember that I never learned to make choices. Everything was always decided for me. Mom planned out every single day for me, and every day was filled to the brim with activities, mostly constructive ones of course. I have been just the opposite with my son, Brian—in fact, I may have gone too far in the other direction as I've wanted him to make decisions in every area. Now he doesn't understand if I tell him to eat his dinner or do his homework, that these are not options for him! Or it's difficult for him to comprehend if I tell him that his dad and I make decisions as adults and parents and he doesn't have any choice in them. But if I'm firm, he accepts that.

He has to learn a lot more about discipline and authority. I've given him a lot of leeway to allow him to develop and branch out, but now he needs to be able to focus and concentrate. Everything has always come so easily to him that now in first grade when he's learning to read and write, he doesn't want to discipline himself to do something that requires a great deal of effort. I've tried to be honest and candid with him in every way, and he has no problem conveying his feelings to me, to say, 'This hurts me.'

On the other hand, maybe I've sometimes been too controlling with Brian in that I don't like him spending the night at someone else's house. I think children are very much aware of their emerging sexuality and want to explore with each other. I keep an eye on that especially since my son, age six, told me he was 'naked with Heather,' a little girlfriend. At least Brian feels he can talk openly about things like that with me. I never could have with Mom.

When I first decided to stay home with Brian after he was born, I had to keep convincing myself that this wasn't a bad thing. Mom always thought less of women who were just housewives. She thought you should achieve—*be like a man.* Women at that time had just started to reverse the cycle and stay home again then, and I wasn't entirely comfortable with it."

SUSAN EMBARKS ON THE JOURNEY

"Actually, I'm just beginning to do things that are really my choice. I've always done the things I was supposed to, and that's hard to break. Mom gave us skills and I have to thank her for that, but all of us have trouble feeling self-esteem. Our sense of self always hinged on performance, which is a pretty variable thing.

When W. and I were first married, I would try to measure up at times, do everything that was expected of me as a wife, and then at other times I would be rebellious. I still don't like the idea of *having to do things.* I don't like making decisions about what food to serve every night because I don't care that much about food. I'm almost a vegetarian now, and I really don't pay much attention to what I eat except for health reasons. W. loves good food.

I think I'm starting to resolve a lot of issues that have been a source of distress for me. I'm establishing a relationship with my parents on my terms. I've actively done this with Dad. He is physically more available and emotionally too. Recently I bought tickets for a concert series just for the two of us and we go together. That's been a wonderful experience for both of us. And he has a tremendous understanding of Brian, what he's going through with his schoolwork now. He's willing to work through issues rather than just closing them off. My mother is much more close-minded although she has prided herself on being the liberal thinker. He's the flexible one.

But Mom also is growing up, I hope. Last week was the first time she ever opened up to me. There has always been that loving, caring side but we didn't see it much. Mom, for all her apparent self-confidence, was never that good at dealing with people. When she opened her business, she liked me to have the direct contact and she talked with people over the phone. It probably was a question of self-esteem with her too. I've always been able to be myself.

I feel that I'm ready to embark on the rest of the journey, wherever that takes me. As soon as I pass the Bar exam, I will have dealt with that ghost directly. All of the things from the past that have hounded me I will have confronted and dealt with directly. It will be time to put together the puzzle my life has been, all those years of trying to survive. I will be able to burst forth with so much that is in my heart and soul."

SUSAN BREAKS THE CHAIN!

So how has Susan, who expresses her own feelings quickly, directly, and without hesitation, been able to overcome her restrictive upbringing? And how has she learned to trust her own capabilities when every move in her life was directed by Mom? Susan, who used to "hide and sleep" when demands were more than she could handle, has discovered she is a capable, talented person who can dance, sing, drive a truck, tile a bathroom, and earn her own way in the workaday world. And on top of it all, she can be a caring, compassionate person who gives her son and husband respect and affection and builds strong bonds with friends.

What is her secret? She isn't certain, but she knows she has survived many painful tests and has come out on top every time. Not that she hasn't experienced failures along the way. It was tough getting into law school because of her LSAT scores, and she was finally accepted only by one school. Then when she finally overcame that hurdle, she had to make the adjustment to the rigorous demands of reading and comprehending huge volumes of case studies and legal decisions, and her grades were mediocre at first. And how she studied—making laborious notes, never missing a class, spending hours in the library poring over cases. But she persevered, and by her junior and senior years her grades were on a steady upswing, and the work was much less difficult. Susan doesn't give up!

Yet many times in her life she has felt lost and abandoned. The move from a sprawling estate in suburbia to a condemned apartment building was probably the most traumatic of all these experiences. Not only was she forced to leave the boarding school that she loved, but she literally had no place to live, no school, no source of income.

It has taken Susan a long time to come to terms with these losses, but through counseling, a supportive relationship with her husband, and a growing sense of the inner "I," she is beginning to realize that she was not abandoned through any fault of her own. She knows that her mother is a driven, insecure person and that the financial crisis her parents faced was very real, that they had to take drastic steps in order to survive. She wishes that her mother had been able to express her fear and anxiety so that she, Susan, could have gained some insight into a painful experience; that she and her siblings had been allowed some voice in the decision that affected them all so dramatically.

Susan has discovered that direct, honest communication is what works for her in all her relationships. If she is sad or upset, she has to learn to convey her feelings in a positive way, taking responsibility for her own part in conflicts and discussing problems without blame or criticism. It isn't easy, but Susan knows she has to be less demanding, less controlling, more caring and accepting!

She is determined that her small son will grow up in an affectionate, nurturing atmosphere, where there is room for fun and play. She encourages him to express his feelings and his natural creative bent, but she has to be careful that this freedom is balanced with discipline.

Now she is in the process of resolving her relationship with both parents, and it is a healing experience that sustains a growing sense of self-worth. Her mother, for the first time, will admit occasionally that she misses her daughter although she neglects even now to keep in touch often. Susan watches with delight as her father and son develop a strong masculine tie; she herself is experiencing the camaraderie with her father that she missed during her turbulent adolescent years.

Susan's Secret Formula:

1. Resolve feelings about your parents and break out of the bitterness and anger of the family coalitions and conflict.
2. Communicate directly and honestly (without being cruel) with family and friends.
3. Value your own achievements—then you'll be able to value those of others. Learn that you aren't perfect, and that no one else is either!
4. Offer love, encouragement, and support to your husband, child, and friends, but set limits—don't permit boundary invasions or make them.

Unraveling the Tangled Skein

Susan recently passed the Bar exam and succeeded at the rigorous test she set for herself. Now she is certain, she will "unravel the tangled skein her life has been" and "burst forth with creativity." And already the tangled skein is unraveling. In the process of defining herself, working out broken relationships, forming new friendships, and planning an original television series for children, she is branching out in every direction, creating new and original patterns.

Growing up in a flexible household, with an open, loving relationship between his parents, Brian will, in all probability, develop into a strong, thoughtful person, with a high level of independence and maturity or *differentiation of self*. He in turn will pass on a sense of self and a caring, compassionate attitude onto his own children, and they onto theirs. Like Laura, Ellen, Amy, Shelley, Kate, Barbara, Marie, and Sophia, Susan has broken the chain!

> . . . The road is cupped
> yellow lilies, crimson clover,
> purple vetch,
> and I am all powerful woman.
> I slip over bridges, across
> wrinkled green oceans,
> grasping planets of ice
> and stars in my fists.
> Wearing the flung peaks
> of mountains
> I see beyond hills,
> beyond thickets,
> night-sprinkled horizons.
> Twelve healthy dragons
> breathe my blue fire.
>
> —"All Powerful Woman"

9

Into My Woman Skin

A strange season.
I have swallowed the rhododendron,
seeds and all.
I have swallowed dense leaves,
dark flexible limbs.
I cry easily, I see
the blank side of the moon
turned to Africa or Asia,
subterranean burrowers, silken
rabbits, blind satin bodies of moles.

A strange winter.
I have turned and twisted,
tunneling under dry leaves,
wet dirt embossed
with pebbles and sand.
I have climbed into dank lairs
of gophers, black as stones.
I have slipped off my skin,
I grow dark leather paws,
long teeth, ancient claws.
I have lived
in the labyrinths of beavers,
caves of she bears.

A strange spring.
I have swallowed
the rhododendron, roots and all.
A delicate translucence blooms in my eyes.
I see clear to the bone blue

core of shrubs, fused veins of maples,
slow silver hearts of rivers.
I see light lighting my fingers,
light in the ribs of my heart,
I slip into my woman skin.

—"Into My Woman Skin"

Born in a small village in Bavaria, Greta was only a few weeks old
when her mother died. The father, a weak, ineffectual man, had no
idea of how to cope with running a household and taking care of his
two daughters, one age ten, and the other a baby.

A STRUGGLE FROM THE BEGINNING

In her resonant voice, with its lightly accented overtones, Greta relates, "My stepmother tried to blame my father for whatever went
wrong in the family. My grandmother blamed my stepmother and my
father. I was blamed for the death of my mother since she died from
problems at childbirth. I was told by friends that for the longest time
after I was born, the family pushed me into the corner and shunted
me aside as if I didn't exist.

The nurturing person for me was my wet nurse. I was allergic to
cow's milk, and the wet nurse (who had a baby of her own) took care
of me. I remember the warmth of her household when I visited her
once when I was maybe two or three years old. We also had maids in
the house who took care of me and women who had been friends of
my mother came by to see me and to check on my well-being. I formed
attachments to them."

FAIRY TALES AND THE EVIL STEPMOTHER

"My first stepmother came into the home as a caretaker-nurse when
my mother was ill. I was always a little afraid of her and never liked
her although she preferred me to her own child, a boy. She had always wanted a girl. This stepmother died of leukemia when I was five.
The next stepmother came in as a nurse for the second wife.

I didn't like either stepmother. I was frightened of the first one,
and the second one was a Prussian, very Teutonic. She was stoic and

strict. However, she would come down with terrible migraines, and the migraines were her weapon for manipulating my sister and me. That's how she got her power—the possibility of the migraines. She would threaten to tell my father if I did anything to displease her and suggest that my behavior had brought on the painful headaches.

My stepbrother was three years younger. We got along fine and I was fond of him, although he had a personality similar to his mother and could be a devious little fellow.

I had a diary when I was about eleven. I wrote in it and later abandoned it. I had a key to it, but my stepmother somehow got hold of it and read it. I kept a journal again at boarding school, but it was mostly a record of my activities.

I was allowed to have my own possessions up to a point, but my stepmother had no respect for anything of mine. When I went off to boarding school, she disposed of all my belongings, which were kept in a big trunk in my bedroom. I was very angry, but I probably couldn't have taken them with me anyway when I had to leave. I don't know if she read my letters. I never felt that I had any say about what I wanted. She would tell me what to wear, what to say, how to think. She was very domineering.

I wanted no part of her—my stepmother. Once when I was only about eight, she asked me if I loved her, and I told her that I didn't. Even then I couldn't play games, be deceitful; I had to be honest with myself and others. I felt uncomfortable and not at all close to either my stepmother or my father. We could never talk about ideas or express feelings. My sister and I talked openly when we could about our feelings, but she was ten years older and away from home from the time I was a little girl.

The rules then for bringing up children were authoritarian. My father was not a tyrant, but my stepmother ran the household. He blustered but didn't convey authority. If I needed rescuing, he didn't do it."

ATTACHMENTS—WHEN YOU HAVE TO MAKE YOUR OWN

Greta, like Shelley, appears to defy everything we know of *attachment theory*—the early bonding between mother and child that Mahler, Bowlby, and others believe to be vital to the physical and emotional development of the infant. We can trace very little in the way of nurturing attachments—the "wet nurse," who gave the infant Greta warmth and affection along with physical nurturance, a sister who loved her but lived far away, a few maids who were sympathetic and listened to her problems—yet essentially Greta was on her own.

But probably Greta, like Shelley, Amy, and Susan, was naturally a resilient individual at birth and was gifted with those traits that defend the inner self—qualities of resourcefulness and strength that appear to be an inborn characteristic for the resilient child. And if we look closely, there were a few early influences that helped give her affection and encouragement. The wet nurse who came in to feed and take care of her when her mother died provided a first sense of closeness and was possibly an even more powerful influence than Greta remembers. She liked to talk with the maids in the household, and they listened and were sympathetic. Her older sister was a consistent mentor for her and continued to offer her deep affection and support throughout her brief life.

Later Greta would reach out for companionship, encouragement, and guidance wherever she could find it—with teachers, school staff, and friends. The island boarding school where she would live during her formative adolescent years instilled in her a strong sense of personal responsibility and compassion for others, and further broadened her love of the arts and the outdoors.

TRAGEDY—AN EARLY PART OF LIFE

"My grandmother lived with us in the second house where we moved when I was eight. In fact, this was her house. We moved in with her when my aunt (her daughter) committed suicide. It was a terrible thing.

My aunt, who was my mother's sister, had wanted to work. Her husband died young, and even though there was enough money to support her, she wanted an outlet for her time and energy. But her brothers wouldn't allow it. Men had a lot of power in those days. I don't know all the reasons for the suicide, but her daughter, my cousin, died with her mother. My grandmother was naturally embittered. The remaining child, a son, was shunted around from one home to another in the family. I felt like an orphan, but he definitely *was* one."

Greta's voice softens until it's almost inaudible, recalling these tragic events. She does not explain how her aunt committed suicide or how her cousin died with her, and I don't ask. I don't want to pry into these painful memories that still cause so much grief some sixty or more years later.

Composing herself, Greta once again radiates strength and the kind of deep courage that characterizes her. She relates,

"By necessity as a child I realized I had to rely on myself. My mother and my first stepmother died. Then my aunt and Cousin Sara were gone. Sara and I were just a year apart, and we had always been together from my earliest recollections. I would go home with her and she with me until finally someone would have to come to get one of us since we lived in separate households. When she died, I experienced a sadness and loneliness that never went away completely.

There was no bonding in our household. Neither my father nor my stepmother ever talked about personal problems. There was too much division between them, and neither of them wanted to take a look at something so frightening as anger or resentment. I think my father sensed that I didn't want to be close to either one of them, and he didn't want that either. I got my affection from other people. The family would go for Sunday walks together in the woods, yet there was no sense of affection or togetherness. This was just something you did as a family because it was expected.

I wouldn't say that I was treated with respect by my stepmother or father. Some teachers in my primary school gave me respect, and there were teachers and fellow students after that who were understanding. My sister listened to my problems and so did some of the maids. I would tell them what was bothering me when I washed dishes with them—a small haven for me. My stepmother didn't like that. She was jealous or afraid of someone saying something against her. One maid frightened me by telling me scary stories about stepmothers, and she was forced to leave."

INVASIONS—AGAIN AND AGAIN

There was little real communication between Greta's parents and *individual boundaries were rigid* between the two daughters and father and stepmother, as both parents appeared to be incapable of real intimacy and affection in any of their relationships. Greta's ties with her sister were close and loving, but the two sisters were far apart in age and in physical environments. There was little expression of ideas in this restrictive family setting and real feelings were suspect. The family maintained *rigid external boundaries* as well, with little allowed outside its fixed borders that were extended only to include the father's nuclear family, his mother, brothers, sister and her children.

Boundary invasions were a part of Greta's life from very early on—*invasions of her privacy, the denial of her right to express her ideas, a total indifference to her love of a few cherished belongings.* The household was a strict authoritarian one where the rules were made by the tyrannical stepparent, with the weak father standing in the background, apparently helpless. And Greta had no privacy, no right to her few possessions. Her diary was never safe from the prying eyes of the stepmother, who had so little regard for Greta's ties to her few possessions, books, dolls, small scraps of jewelry, that she gave everything away when Greta went off to boarding school.

"I made a few friends when I was younger," Greta relates, "but no lasting ones until I became a student at boarding school. I was never comfortable about bringing friends home as I had to help with the cleaning and other household duties. I could never play until I had done my chores. When I was quite young and we had servants, I didn't have as many responsibilities, but in the crash of '29 my father lost a great deal, and we couldn't afford a maid.

Before the crash came he had sent us to Austria, thinking we would be safer. All the people from Germany were thought of as the 'poor people from Germany.' We were very much affected by the crash. Financial worries added even more turmoil to an already troubled home. My father tended to splurge rather than plan. I never had an allowance—it didn't exist. Sometimes I would have a little money from relatives and friends to go to fairs and occasional movies.

I taught myself how to tie my own shoes and button my sweaters. I don't think I ever asked for much because there was no one to ask. My stepmother had a way of making me feel ashamed if I did. I had friends who had older sisters—they would show me how to make up a bed and tuck in the corners, for instance. I wanted to be independent, and I found a way to do that. When I was told 'you can't,' I would find another way. I did well in elementary school until emotional problems started to get in the way. I began to get headaches, my grades were dropping and I knew it was time to leave. I had an instinctive feeling for it."

SETTING BOUNDARIES

Greta sensed intuitively that her stepmother was an arrogant person who would attempt to invade every aspect of her life. Recognizing that the inner "I" was in real danger of extinction, she set up strong barriers against intrusion. She learned to be independent and competent, to do for herself. Growing up in a suffocating family atmosphere, she refused to placate her stepmother with lies and deceit, by pretending to love this person she instinctively disliked.

She was firm in setting limits in her relationships with others as well. "I was only eight years old," Greta relates, "when I began to feel uncomfortable with my Sunday school teacher. He was holding me in his lap too long and touching me in a way I disliked. I sensed something strange and I stopped going to church. No amount of persuasion could get me to go back until he left."

NATURE AND THE INNER SELF

Greta also found a strong and spontaneous bond with nature even as a small girl. She discovered space for herself, both physically and emotionally, in the beautiful wooded areas near her home. The walks under the trees and through the winding paths gave her an opportunity for reflection and solitude.

"I had to create my own environment and shape my own world," she says. "I would take long walks in the woods. We lived in a small town about twenty miles from the nearest city. The village was housed between a hill and a mountain—not quite a mountain, more than a hill—in southwest Germany. It was a resort area famous for vineyards and very beautiful. People came there to recover from illnesses in the sanitarium and at the health resorts. We enjoyed a temperate climate in a lovely area shielded by mountains from the north and west at the end of the Rhine plains. Almond and fig trees grew there.

I took the right to be alone for myself in the hills, meadows, and woods. I had a dog then. He would bark when the Nazi troops were marching by, and they took care of that—they poisoned him! This was in the early thirties. The Nazi movement started early, much earlier than most people realize.

I always loved sports and physical activities. I remember running— such a beautiful feeling. I felt my body was a machine, and I could do with it whatever I wanted. Since we lived on the outskirts of town, I had to bike or run whenever I went into town. All of this was a big part, I think, of keeping in touch with myself, my freedom, my independence. I thought I could run across rivers and mountains, trotting like a small pony over fields and woods and streams, and when the Nazis were moving in on me, I did! A sense of being at home in nature helped me going from one country to another because I felt the trees and meadows were always the same everywhere. The natural beauty of the outdoors gave me a feeling of comfort and balance.

I don't think my survival was so much looking out for myself as feeling that I needed to think for myself—*seize the moment.* I had an instinct for that when I was young or I wouldn't have been so emphatic about leaving home at twelve for boarding school. My stepmother constantly belittled me and I had to escape from her tirades. This was one of her ways of exerting power. I would rush outside to walk in the woods for solace."

A LIFELINE AT TWELVE—BOARDING SCHOOL

Without ever fully understanding why, Greta made a crucial decision at age twelve. The atmosphere in her home was one of denial and repression, verging on paranoia. Greta had few friends and there was no time for talk or play. Even Greta's strong spirit was beginning to falter under the strain of living a straitened life; her grades were falling, and she knew it was time to escape. Boarding school would prove to be an experience that both strengthened her character and allowed her creative nature to thrive.

"My sister left home early, at around thirteen, and when I reached age twelve, I too asked to leave. I was being suffocated—my ideas, feelings, everything. My father didn't have much say about anything. He did a lot of posturing and blustering, but all of us knew it didn't mean anything. I had to find my role models elsewhere and I did.

By that time I desperately needed rescuing. I knew that I had to get away—knew it absolutely! My sister, who always stayed in touch with me, encouraged me to go. She understood how I felt because she had undergone the same experience. My stepmother and father didn't want me to leave, probably because of the expense. But my uncle knew someone who taught at my school, and he talked to my father and made the arrangements for me.

My boarding school was located in the north of Germany on a small island. It became my salvation. This was a positive experience in every way, a progressive school that was experimental in its teaching methods, with an emphasis on art and creativity. You were motivated by the example of others and by what interested you. There were a lot of things that did interest me—sports, the humanities, painting—and I was free to express myself.

I didn't go home often on vacations. I was glad to be away. Sometimes I stayed with my friends and sometimes I visited my sister, who was now studying to become a doctor. Home was quite a distance away, and traveling was not that easy."

SETTING LIMITS

Boarding school at first appeared to be a Utopia for Greta, with its emphasis on self-expression. But danger lurked around the corner, and Greta again had to stand up for herself, as she had so many times in the past. This time the pressures were greater and more critical because of the growing power of the totalitarian fascist state.

Yet her long rambles over the island and her vigorous outside work, keeping up the gardens for the school, were a way of reinforcing a sense of self. They not only offered Greta a time for pleasure and intense reflection, but fortified her strong, youthful body for the trials ahead. Since she naturally loved sports, she threw herself into basketball and running track with the same fervor and enthusiasm she put into all phases of her life.

At twelve, on going away to school, she learned how easily we shed all our material belongings and how little they matter in the long run. "Possessions weren't important to me," Greta says. "I felt from very early on that wherever I went I would take the 'I' with me and that was all that mattered. When I fled I couldn't take anything with me, but they couldn't take the 'I.' Whatever was there was strong inside and the rest didn't matter."

IMPENDING DANGER: THE NAZI MOVEMENT

On the long, perilous journey ahead Greta would need every ounce of the courage and spirit that had served her so well so far. The era was the late thirties, Greta was sixteen, and there were ominous signs of repression and persecution. Even in the idyllic setting of her school, Nazi influences were beginning to seep into the atmosphere.

"We were forced to have a Hitler youth group at the school. I was part of the student council, and some of the youngsters tried to edge me out because I was Jewish. I told them they could all resign but I wouldn't. I learned to fight. Of course I had been fighting all along, but now it was a matter of real survival. Those were terrible times.

I had good teachers who offered me direction. They gave me assignments that built up my strength, keeping me involved in looking after others. I would get a call from the head of the school, asking if I would room with a girl who needed special help. This happened several times—that I roomed with women who were younger or had problems. The school was wise. They must have felt this is what I needed, and it's a lesson that has stood me in good stead.

I lived there at the school from age twelve until seventeen, first with a married couple and then in the dorms. It was lovely setting, not far from the Dutch border, a long narrow island surrounded by bay and ocean. I stayed outdoors a lot and helped maintain the property for the school. This was an integral part of what I learned.

Thanks to the wonderful influences of my school and my sister, Rita, I did develop a sense of who I was. Rita was a strong person, very clever and capable but understanding and compassionate at the same time. She was my role model except that, unfortunately, we were separated from the time that I was five. I was too young to be a threat to my stepmother, but she felt my sister, a beautiful young woman, was a rival for my father's attention and affection. So my sister went away to boarding school and after that, studied medicine. I managed to see her on vacations as often as I could.

She became a doctor, which wasn't unusual for women in Germany at that time. But one of her professors at Freibourg where she was studying warned a group of students of danger from the Nazis. These students had been outspoken in their opposition to the Gestapo rule, and the professor advised them to get out of the country as fast as possible. My sister hiked over the mountains into Switzerland and then went to France from Switzerland. She studied in Switzerland and worked as a doctor at clinics in France but never had her own practice. The Nazis saw to that."

ESCAPE—WITH TIN CANS FOR SHOES

"After I finished boarding school I was visiting my sister in France. I couldn't get a permit to stay so I had to go back to Berlin, where I had been working. I had a room in a private home there, and when I stopped by to see my father before going back, I found a postcard from the landlady saying that there had been 'visitors' looking for me. I knew instantly what that meant!

My stepmother wasn't Jewish so she didn't have to worry, and my father didn't believe anything could happen to him. Although I had tried to persuade him to escape immediately, he felt he was too old to make the change. He was caught later and put in one of the death camps. I tried to get my little stepbrother out, but in the frenzy to leave I couldn't take him with me. I left then and there.

I intended to go to Holland so my suitcase went by train there. I never arrived because I heard people were being stopped at the border. I managed to get to France, where my sister was living. She had married and had two small children. I walked for days and slept in the woods or any isolated place I could find at night. My shoes wore out so I flattened tin cans and walked on them. Luckily, I was strong and fit from all the walking and running I'd done and from all my athletic activities at school.

I finally crossed the border into France, but the Nazis caught up with me even there when the Vichy government took over. I was interned in France for many months. The Germans were about twenty kilometers away at that point, but with the help of a sympathetic French official who signed for me to leave, I was released.

That camp in France was a gathering point from which people were shipped to the death camps. I had been looking out for two other young women, and when they were released, I felt I should go. The authorities called me in for questioning three times, and I thought I would be permitted to join my sister again. I tried desperately, but the third time I couldn't get back to her. My sister never escaped, and despite all the plans we had made for me to take her two children, I couldn't get them out either."

ACTS OF COURAGE: THE TENOR OF A LIFE

Greta states these terrible events simply and without apparent emotion, and although I don't know all the details of the perilous trip across Germany into France or of the internment in the Vichy camp, I don't want to ask. But to even think of such losses—her father, sister, the two children, the sister's husband—is so staggering that it's almost impossible to comprehend. Yet acts of courage and fortitude have set the tenor for Greta's entire life—as a child, as a young woman, and today.

Such losses have taken a toll on Greta despite her strength and resiliency. It's difficult for her to always maintain her persona of optimism and hope. But she struggles to maintain an emotional balance, refusing to give in to self-pity and bitterness. According to Erikson, the more we move away from the demands of the ego and are concerned with doing for others—*in the true altruistic sense of helping without expecting anything in return*—the more fulfilled we are. And Greta, from the time of her childhood and boarding school days, has been concerned with reaching out, embracing others.

Child psychologist E. Staub theorizes that when a child feels secure, as a consequence of warmth and nurturing in the early childhood years, this feeling of safety and security minimizes concern with self and allows for the development of *empathy* and willingness to help others. Greta experienced little warmth or affection during childhood or adolescence, so it's difficult to account for her strongly sympathetic nature. Certainly the influence of *mentors* in her life was a significant factor—the relationship with her sister, a wise and courageous woman—and the outstanding staff and teachers of the boarding school where Greta found guidance and direction.

When we move too far in one direction and focus on the problems of others to such an extent that we try to control their lives and fail to resolve our own issues, this is *caretaking*. But Greta's willingness to sacrifice herself for others was a life-giving force for her as well as for those she befriended and may have helped save her sanity!

SETTING BOUNDARIES: THE BATTLE GOES ON

"I still have to struggle with protecting my boundaries. I've had to fight with my husband to be my own person. It's an insecurity, I think, the male power thing. When I was married and first came to the United States, I was used to living as *I wanted to* in France. My husband, D., didn't like the way I dressed, the way I spoke. He wanted me to be instantly American, which of course I couldn't do. I fought his ideas for me every step of the way. I keep fighting. He feels uncomfortable when I slip something over my pajamas and take a walk at night or when I talk to strangers. Just by eye contact I seem to initiate a conversation without intending to be intrusive. D. is a conservative person, and I am unconventional, but I have to be myself. I wouldn't hold *him* back in any way.

My unconventional streak doesn't create a problem for my children. My daughter might be a little embarrassed if I do something out of the ordinary. But it's a good relationship, and we talk about problems and sort them out. My son doesn't seem to mind except sometimes if I try to hold his hand when we're out together.

For the past several years I have been volunteering with Hospice, and I find I have to maintain boundaries in my work too. I have a client I've worked with for over a year. At one point she wanted to know if she [was a] client or friend, and I had to think that out because I thought she had overstepped the relationship a little. If I let that happen, I'm not effective. If the patient doesn't recognize boundaries for herself, I have to set them. We resolved the issue in that she (the client) has my phone number for emergencies but doesn't use it otherwise."

BECOMING A POET

"I had painted for years, but I didn't start writing poetry until a few years ago. I came down with a toxic thyroid condition very suddenly. Because of this thyroid imbalance, emotionally everything steps into overdrive. Your whole system goes berserk, and you feel frenetic and driven. You have to have either surgery or medication, and medication worked for me. This was in the late seventies. Some people experience an intense creative period as I did, and I started writing and couldn't stop. But when the chemistry is balanced through medication, you generally lose that drive. I never did. It's a kind of miracle.

My husband didn't take my writing seriously at first. He couldn't understand it. He would correct my spelling and my syntax. Now I'm taking theater workshops as well as working with small theater groups. I still get objections from him, but I continue with them. The theater does take up much of my time, learning lines, and I have to concentrate. He felt I was neglecting other things, yet I feel I have to learn how to connect with my audience. The performing and writing are both part of the creative process. The idea and the response. The writer and the listener."

PIECING THE PUZZLE

What then are Greta's secrets as she moves into her seventh decade but continues to expand and develop new and challenging horizons? She seems to have a relatively clear picture of the puzzle, and this is how she puts it together for us:

1. "Seize the day"—live in and for the moment.
2. Guard your borders—Defend yourself against anyone who encroaches on the right to express yourself.
3. Maintain boundaries in your professional life—Don't allow your professional concerns to intrude on your personal life or your personal life on your professional life.
4. Stay in touch with the sources that grant you solace and vision—nature, poetry, art, music.

Seize the Day

What does Greta mean when she talks of "seizing the moment"? According to Erikson, the ability to live in the present—neither dwelling in the past nor living for the future—is one of the great foundations for a healthy emotional outlook. When we live in the present, we focus on what is happening to us now, at this very minute, and in this way we experience it completely. We see, we feel, we taste, we touch, we hear *now!* We are alive!

In a sense we might speculate that Greta has been forced to live for today as her past entailed chiefly suffering and pain, and the future, very possibly, didn't even exist! Yet Greta could easily have become narrow and embittered and spent the rest of her life dwelling on past tragedies. Or she might have envisioned an illusory happy future that held little relationship to the real world.

Seize the moment has deeper implications for Greta. She appears to have recognized instinctively the danger signals in her life and understood how to act on them—leaving home for boarding school, escaping from the Nazis, both at crucial turning points in her life.

Guard Your Borders

Daily we grapple with conflicts. How far can we go in asserting our own choices? Are we selfish when we take actions that we feel are necessary to our emotional well-being? Greta, though strong and spirited, is not impervious to self-doubt. Recently she moved from a home she had cherished, with a network of friends and activities, to a senior complex in another state that offered health facilities for her husband. The move was not her choice, and even now she grapples with feelings of uncertainty and displacement that are difficult for her to resolve. But she is moving on, building ties to this new community, working with children in the schools, joining drama and poetry groups.

Maintain Boundaries in Your Professional Life

In her hospice work Greta insists on maintaining the invisible (but very real) division between patient and counselor. If the relationship becomes too intimate, she knows she will lose the objectivity and wisdom that make her valuable to the families she works with. But it's necessary to set these limits again and again in every different setting and circumstance.

Stay with the Sources That Grant You Solace and Vision

Paradoxically, Greta's thyroid condition drew her into the life of a writer! Typically, she turned an adverse situation into a fulfilling one, using the tremendous energy that came with a physical imbalance to embark on a new creative pursuit—the writing of poetry. Yet once the condition was corrected, the dedication to her new avocation stayed with her as a treasured aspect of her life. Possibly the love of poetry and the will to express herself imaginatively have always been a part of her nature, but were never explored until she was suddenly faced with this implosion of frenetic energy. And her long walks in the woods in every season reinforce for her a deep sense of solace and continuity.

GENERATIVITY AND CREATIVITY: THE FORCES THAT SUSTAIN US

A survivor of the Holocaust and a traumatic childhood, Greta appears to have been gifted from the beginning with a natural sense of self. Almost from birth, when her mother died, she has had to fend for herself—to form attachments when few were offered, to defend herself from emotional deprivation and repression from two stepmothers, to survive against all odds.

Greta's courage and confidence have stood her in good stead, since her life has been one of immense challenges that could have easily led to illness, insanity, or even death. We might add *especially death*, for Greta managed to escape capture and genocide—not once but many times over. Certainly, all of her wits, intelligence, and courage were essential for her to survive the horrors of Hitler's concentration camps. Her entire family perished in those death camps or were victims of Nazi brutality. A history of losses.

Yet finding solace and solitude in nature, relying on a strong sense of the "I" that she carries with her on every journey, Greta personifies Erikson's characterization of *generativity and creativity* in the later years. The alternative is a period of *stagnation and despair* as we confront the illnesses and losses of old age. Caring for others and the pursuit of creativity—in art, music, dance, drama, poetry, gardening, and cooking—are Erikson's answer to the challenges of aging.

Greta illustrates the rare capacity of the human spirit to triumph over adversity. Imbued with warmth, compassion, and vision, she radiates strength from a deep inner core. Hardships, far from making her into a narrow, embittered person, only seem to have enlarged her amazing spirit. Even at the worst of times she has turned from her own plight to take care of others. And throughout all the suffering and danger, she has retained her vitality as artist, teacher, poet, and counselor.

Greta, like Laura, Amy and Ellen, like Shelley, Kate, Barbara, Marie, Peggy, Sophia, and Susan, has suffered abandonment, loss, and hardship. But all of these women are daily exploring, building, finding new avenues of expression, developing a stronger sense of the inner self. And Greta "shines above the shadows," illumining the way for all of us who travel dark paths alone.

> . . . So much, so much
> is gone without a trace,
> you rake the leaves and still
> the crackling piles grow taller, wider
> across the lawn,
> spiders flaunt their intricate designs
> for holding on, retrenching,
> a stubborn dust grows back
> on every polished table.
>
> You forget to count
> how many times
> you baked the rising cake
> to find it fallen,
> how many times you soothed
> the bleeding knee
> to find the tall blond bodies
> of your children springing past you,
>
> and clearly you can see
> the masks you borrow to survive

wear many faces
each broken act of tenderness
some call love
repeats the cycle
yet footprints in the snow
now drifted over
were surely there
to bring the lost calf in
before the long door opens.

—"Cycles"

10
Conclusion

Building on a framework of family systems concepts, I began my study of family dynamics by considering the implications of boundary violations on women—any emotional, physical, or sexual violation of the feminine self. My chief aim was to explore the emotional reverberations of boundary invasions in childhood on the developmental process.

My study was based, not on clinical tests, but on the testimony of women who spoke articulately and candidly about the forces that shaped and shook them, the difficulties and pain they faced in changing negative patterns of denial and dependency. In analyzing their narratives within the context of family systems theory, I attempted to discover the processes at work in the evolution from dependency and emotional reactivity (or undifferentiation of self) to independence, balance, and discipline (or differentiation of self). In my research I have been not so much concerned with the journey's destination as with its valleys, mountains, and streams—*the paths that mark the passage.*

My focus has never been a militant one, but I write from a woman's perspective—because I am a woman and because women in our society, traditionally and historically, have been trained since birth to be tolerant, submissive, and self-sacrificing. Such characteristics are virtues of the nurturing woman, but unless they are coupled with a healthy respect for the self, they may lead to martyrdom and victimization. When we add to that cultural message of submission, backgrounds of pathology, alcoholism, poverty, and patriarchy, the woman may lose all sense of identity and become vulnerable and insecure. She may even slip into the abyss of mental illness, addiction, or deviant behavior.

One of my chief concerns was to discover if longtime invasions in the form of sexual, physical or emotional abuse might lead to severe wounds of the psyche and into the darkened woods of pathology or addiction. As the project progressed, I discovered that the women who participated in my study had each arrived at singularly different points in their journey toward the light, and that, yes, not one of them has escaped unscarred.

The losses inflicted by destructive family processes are well hidden in my subjects, who are, for the most part, accomplished, poised women. Yet Laura still battles periods of anxiety, self-doubt, and chronic back pain that may well be a by-product of the traumas of childhood. Shelley, coming from a background of severe neglect and deprivation, undergoes bouts of intense depression that strike without warning with the force of a hot branding iron. Sophia, whose childhood was usurped by her mother, experiences sudden shifts in mood from elation to depression and must constantly guard against slipping into predatory relationships. The list goes on and on—depression, physical pain, dependency, perfectionism, volatile mood swings, the fragile emotional balance—all of these and more are the bitter legacy of the dysfunctional childhood.

Yet the surprising finding of my study is that few of these women have followed downward paths into pathology. It's true that Julia has slipped further and further into the black caverns of despair and depression, and that Marie, the victim of long-term sexual abuse by an alcoholic father, needs ongoing therapy and the constant support of her AA group to sustain her emotional well-being and to keep her from slipping back into the escape through addiction. Kate, still attempting to create order in an unstable world, must constantly fight against deep-seated feelings of insecurity and her need for control and perfectionism.

All of these women have suffered setbacks and detours on the journey and have, for the most part, undergone counseling or intensive therapy to remove themselves from the emotional chaos, neglect, or bitterness of the nuclear family. But primarily they are survivors— resourceful, resilient survivors who have overcome enormous odds. For not only have most of them transcended legacies of neglect, abuse, rejection, violence, and persecution, but they have become strong compassionate human beings in the process. In the stories of these women are paths that lead into the clearing and the light, to Shelley's village of sunlight that is "liquid gold."

What are their secrets? Human beings are complex and the experiences and factors that shape them appear intricate and interwoven, but in citing the traits that distinguish the survivors in my study, I would name *honesty, courage, compassion,* and *creativity.*

Coming as most of them do from a background of half truths, myths, and outright lies, these women place a singular value on honesty. They have seen firsthand the confusion and frustration caused by denial, repression, and magical thinking. Now on observing behavior that mocks and destroys, they know, *this causes me pain or anger or sadness.* On hearing ridicule or blame, they are aware, *this hurts me.* On seeing a pattern in their own lives that repeats the destructive processes of their childhood, they can say, *I want to change; Can I? How do I begin?*

Many of us resist change even when we hate our own untenable and miserable experiences in the old stuck mold. We resist because change threatens, pushes us out of old, comfortable ways, shoves us forward into taking risks. But it was courage that enabled Laura to leave with three small children and start a new life in a strange city, courage that gave Greta the strength to escape through the woods and fields of Nazi Germany with only tin cans for shoes, courage that gave Susan the fortitude to survive in an abandoned tenement. In fact, each of these women has had the courage to make difficult, unpopular choices, to survive under fire, to refuse to give up.

In resolving the search for identity Erikson suggests that in the second stage of adulthood we look to the forces of generativity and the wish to bear and nurture children. In a larger sense we extend that nurturing spirit to the community and to future generations through caring for others. Amy demonstrates her capacity for compassionate idealism in her concern for "everyone she meets" and recently in her new role as mother to a baby son; Greta's focus today is on teaching children and fostering in them a lifelong love of language and poetry. Shelley is actively working with organizations that promote the rights and welfare of children and women in need. Laura is building a strong relationship with her mother and bringing her bright spirit into the lives of her grandchildren.

Paradoxically, the painful struggle to define the self appears to have enriched understanding and nourished art and creativity. The paradox, according to psychotherapist and spiritual teacher, Jack Kornfield, is that often the experiences that nurture the spirit evolve from our greatest limitations and difficulties! For it is through hardship, pain, and challenge that we grow in every dimension.

Shelley prophesies that if she had led a normal, unchallenging childhood, she might have become an "overweight housewife eating chocolates" instead of the accomplished scholar and author she has become. Sophia is aware that her "demons" have fed her art, made her music richer and more complex. Ellen, now that she has become poet, performer, and musical apprentice, "feels empowered in so many ways." Susan delights in raising her young son, is studying piano for the first time, and "is ready to embark on the rest of the journey." Barbara, with two published books to her credit, has a "light that shines inside" and that light "has taught her to sing" a joyful message.

This is the message of empowerment that every woman can read. As women and as individuals we give ourselves power through recognition of our boundaries, through their valiant defense, through learning to say yes or no. We give ourselves power by setting limits and enforcing the consequences when limits are not observed, through affirmation and belief in ourselves. Then we are ready, like Susan, to "burst forth with creativity . . . in heart and soul."

I think it is appropriate to close with stanzas from a poem that describe a glimpse of the joy I feel—we all feel—at times of discovery and recognition. The lake at Cape Cod, with its iridescent noon waters, is a place and a time like that, a place where *the world surprises me* and *I can walk on water.*

> . . . Tufted marshweed
> protrudes at water's edge,
> transparencies so clear
> one foot, two feet deep,
> I touch patterns sleeping
> on a bed in motion.
> Light balances between,
> above shallow ripples
> curves out in broken lengths
> glittering like bracelets.
>
> Though I can't surprise
> the lake,
> the lake surprises me
> with burning shadows,
> fickle patterns, fire on foam.

Without wishing, planning
visions leaps
beyond perimeters.
As easily as skiers
tracing feathered spume,
the spirit chooses me
and I can walk on water.

—"Lake Poem I"

Bibliography

Ainsworth, M.D.S., M. Behar, E. Waters, and S. Wall (1978). *Patterns of attachment*. Hillsdale, NJ: Erlbaum.

Anonymous. (1981). *Twelve steps and twelve traditions*. New York: Alcoholics Anonymous World Services.

Bandura, A. (1977). *Social learning theory*. Englewood Cliffs, NJ: Prentice-Hall.

Barrett, M. J., and T. S. Trepper (1992). Unmasking the incestuous family. *Networker* 16, 139–161.

Baumrind, D. (1971). Current patterns of parental authority. *Developmental Psychology Monograph* 4, no. 1, part 2.

Beattie, M. (1990). *The language of letting go*. Center City, MN: Hazelden.

Bee, H. (1989). *The developing child* (5th ed.). New York: HarperCollins.

Blakeslee, S. (August 29, 1995). In brain's early growth timetable may be crucial. *New York Times*, C1–C3.

Boss, P., and J. Greenberg (1984). Family boundary ambiguity. *Family Process* 23, 535–545.

Bowen, M. (1978). *Family therapy in clinical practice*. New York: Jason Aronson.

Bowen, M. (1966). The use of family theory in clinical practice. *Comprehensive Psychiatry*, 345–374.

Bowlby, J. (1969). Attachment. *Attachment and Loss* 1. New York: Basic Books.

Bowlby, J. (1980). Loss, sadness, and depression. *Attachment and Loss* 3. New York: Basic Books.

Crain, W. C. (1985). *Theories of development: Concepts and applications* (2nd ed). Englewood Cliffs, NJ: Prentice Hall.

Dunne, J. G. (January 13, 1997). The Humboldt murders. *The New Yorker*, 44–62.

Erikson, E. H. (1959). *Identity and the life cycle*. New York: Norton.

Fontana, V. (1976). *Somewhere a child is crying: Maltreatment, causes, and prevention*. New York: New American Library.

Fossum, M., and M. J. Mason (1986). *Facing shame.* New York: W. W. Norton.

Friel, J., and L. Friel (1988). *Adult children: The secrets of dysfunctional families.* Deerfield Beach: Health Communications.

Haley, J. (1976). *Problem-solving therapy.* San Francisco: Jossey-Bass.

Haley, J. (1963). *Strategies of psychotherapy.* New York: Grune & Stratton.

Hartman, A., and J. Laird (1983). *Family-centered social work practice.* New York: The Free Press.

Hoffman, L. (1975). Enmeshment and the two richly cross-joined systems. *Family Process* 14, 457–467.

Jack, D. C. (1991). *Silencing the self: Women and depression.* Cambridge, MA: Harvard University Press.

Jacobson, E. (1954). The self and the object world. *Psychoanalytic Study of the Child* 9, 75–120.

Janzen, C., and O. Harris (1986). *Family treatment in social work practice.* Itasca, IL: Peacock.

Jensen, L. C. (1985). *Adolescence: Theories, research, applications.* St. Paul: West.

Jung, C. (1933). *Modern man in search of a soul.* New York: Harcourt Brace.

Kornfield, J. (1993). *A path with heart.* New York: Bantam.

Large, T. (1989). Some aspects of loneliness in families. *Family Process* 28, 25–34.

Lenz, F. (1995). *Surfing the Himalayas.* New York: St. Martin's.

Lerner, H. G. (1985). *The dance of anger: A woman's guide to changing the patterns of intimate relationships.* New York: Harper & Row.

Mahler, M. S., F. Pine, and A. Bergman (1975). *The psychological birth of the human infant.* New York: Basic Books.

Minuchin, S. (1978). *Families and family therapy.* Cambridge: Harvard University Press.

Minuchin, S. (1967). *Families of the slums.* New York: Basic Books.

Myers, D. G. (1989). *Psychology.* New York: Worth.

Napier, A. Y., and C. A. Whitaker (1978). *The family crucible.* New York: Harper & Row.

Nichols, M. (1983). *Family therapy: Concepts and methods.* New York: Gardner Press.

Orgat, S. N., K. R. Silk, et al. (1990). Childhood sexual and physical abuse in adult patients with borderline personality disorder. *American Journal of Psychiatry* 147, 1008–1012.

Papp, P., and Imber-Black, E. (1996). Family themes: Transmission and transformation. *Family Process* 35, 5–16.

Patterson, G. R. (1975). *Families: Applications of social learning to family life.* Champaign, IL: Research Press.

Rotter, J. B. (1966). Generalized expectancies for internal versus external control of reinforcement. *Psychological Mongraphs* 80, no. 1.

Satir, V. (1972). *Peoplemaking.* Palo Alto, CA: Science and Behavior Books.

Selvini Palazzoli, M., et al. (1978). *Paradox and counterparadox*. New York: Jason Aronson.

Shurkin, J. N. (1992). *Terman's kids: The ground-breaking study of how the gifted grow up*. Boston: Little Brown.

Smith, M. J. (1981). *When I say no, I feel guilty*. New York: Bantam Books.

Staub, E. (1979). Positive social behavior and morality. *Socialization and Development* 2. New York: Academic.

Talmon, M., and V. Wood (1983). Family boundaries in transition. *Family Process* 22, 347–357.

Terman, L. (1916). *The measurement of intelligence*. Boston: Houghton Mifflin.

Werner, E. E., J. M. Bierman, and F. E. French (1971). *The children of Kauai*. Honolulu: University of Hawaii Press.

Whitaker, C. A., and D. V. Keith (1981). Symbolic-experiential family therapy. In A. S. Gurman and D. P. Kniskern (eds.), *Handbook of family therapy*. New York: Brunner Mazel.

Williamson, J. M., C. M. Bourdin, and B. A. Howe (1991). The ecology of adolescent maltreatment: A multi-level examination of adolescent physical abuse, sexual abuse, and neglect. *Journal of Consulting and Clinical Psychology* 59, 449–457.

Wyatt, G. E., and M. Newcomb (1990). Internal and external mediators of women's sexual abuse in childhood. *Journal of Consulting and Clinical Psychology* 58, 756–767.

Index

About the Author

ANNE COPE WALLACE is a teacher, freelance writer, and award-winning poet who lives in Madison, New Jersey.